Scars of Stars

Israel Ayanfe Ademola **Olubori**

Copyright © 2024, Scars of Stars

All Rights Reserved!

ISBN: 9798345298695

Contact the author: ayanfeolubori66@gmail.com

Disclaimer: The information contained within this book is for informational purposes only and is not to be construed as professional advice.

CONTENTS

Chapter 1 _____ 5

SCARS OF STARS _____ 5

Chapter 2 _____ 15

WILDERNESS _____ 15

Chapter 3 _____ 31

BATTLE LINE _____ 31

Chapter 4 _____ 55

HAEMORRHAGE _____ 55

Chapter 5 _____ 69

THORN IN THE FLESH _____ 69

Chapter 6 _____ 83

AUDACITY OF FAITH _____ 83

Chapter 7 _____ 105

STARDOM _____ 105

Chapter 8 _____ 123

WEAPON OF MASS DESTRUCTION _____ 123

Chapter 9 _____ 137

DOWN BUT NOT OUT _____ *137*

Chapter 10 _____ *145*

HALL OF FAME _____ *145*

Chapter 11 _____ *155*

PANECEA _____ *155*

CHAPTER 1
SCARS OF STARS

Scars are the marks left behind from injuries and wounds sustained from hurts, damages, abuses, trauma and the bad experiences of the past left behind to haunt you or remind you of how far you have gone, how well you have fought the battles and how you get to where you are.

Some were bequeathed greatness and trusted, and a platter of goods was transferred to their laps when many others achieved greatness not by virtue of birth or inheritance but by personal efforts, struggles, fights, failures, and never-ending habits.

Over ninety percent of the present billionaires never inherited their wealth; they attracted wealth, built wealth and sustained the wealth. Most of those who inherited wealth have peculiar problems managing the wealth because those who have never fought against poverty and prevailed would not be able to understand the wisdom of sustainable wealth management. You only conquer or overcome what you passed through; experience will teach you not to fall back into poverty.

Most people at birth are potential stars loading and waiting for the appointed time of manifestations, but many will fade away with time, the dew of life will swallow some up, and the pressure from the forces of darkness will choke some and sniff life out of them.

The battle line is drawn, and only the tough, rugged, deviant fighters who refuse to give up after the fall of defeat can live to illuminate.

There are ordinary stars that do nothing to shine. They are rising stars that appear breathy in the daytime but cannot shine because of the lack of darkness. And there are superstars. So, all stars are different in size, brightness, intensity, and speed.

Invitation to trouble is when you choose not to be ordinary, wish to shine, glow and illuminate. You are caught in trouble and fishing in trouble waters because several forces that have not noticed you before will suddenly revolt against you and launch attacks from different angles to frustrate you to retreat and give up the struggles to be relevant.

First and foremost, you are seen as a force that has come to tamper with the status quo. The forces that be would not want to relinquish power, and authorities will come against you with resistance.

Since nature abhors vacuums for you to rise, shine, and occupy, someone must give way to being displaced or replaced, and the battle will be fierce.

Furthermore, your star will definitely provide illuminations and directions to others around you, and these also have powers wrestling against them not to fulfil purpose; which would then lead to a spiritual gang up against you to frustrate you or eliminate you.

If you tend to rise too early, like Moses in the land of Egypt, the dues of life will choke you and force you to retreat and run for your dear life. This will then propel you to go through your season of preparation and training for greatness in the wilderness of life.

Stargazers are people who foresee the future of stars ahead of the stars themselves and can manipulate or help to actualise the realisation of these stars.

Stars don't shine without darkness; the thicker the darkness, the brighter their star shines, and the stargazers are professionals whose duty is to read and interpret the meaning of each star as it rises. Where there is no opposition, there will be no victory. Stars don't come out at night as many of us think. Stars are always there even during the day but are not relevant until their appointed time and in the conducive atmosphere of gross darkness. All stars need darkness to shine, and that is why we only notice them at night.

Now, if we need darkness to shine, why are we scared of darkness? Stars don't fear darkness; they thrive in it.

"And the light shined in darkness, and comprehended it not" (John 1:5)

This is proof that even Jesus Christ, despite his godly nature, had to submit to the rules of contestants with the power of darkness to shine before fulfilling his purpose.

Notice also that John the Baptist did not jump the gum but waited for his season of manifestations.

Some people are gifted with the gifts of reading and understanding the rise and fall of stars. They know when the great star is born and when another star dies, irrespective of their religion, just a pure gift of God made perfect through the application of knowledge and the understanding of time. The early people who acquired the knowledge of star reading were from the East. They saw the appearance of the star of Jesus and traced the star to Bethlehem.

Let's assume it is the star that appears above, and some people apart from your parent have seen it well ahead of everybody. Not every one of them will come with the gift with a good heart and genuine intentions or with a heart of celebrating you.

"Saying, where is he that is born king of the Jews? For we have seen his star in the east and have come to worship him". (Mathew 2:2)

These made some people happy and made some others crack their brains, calling and assembling powers and authorities to unravel the mystery of the rising star.

"Then Herod, when he had privily called the wise men and enquired of them diligently what time the star appeared" (Mathew 2:7)

Note here that King Herod's interest was not for the good of the star because he was threatened by a little star boy who was just appearing. He was also the man given to knowledge and instructed them to conduct a diligent search for an innocent boy whose star was troubling the powers that ruled the nation.

Furthermore, they were charged with bringing back news of the new rising star who had come to upstage or overthrow the king by establishing a new world order. The plan was to cut them young and stop them from growing. They were also charged with reporting the star's appearance time to destroy him and his infancy.

Every potential cock that will crow will not be caught by the eagle for food; they will survive everything thrown at them from infancy. Sometimes, all it needs is divine intervention through instructions and directions to avert the danger on the way, but sometimes, some order would be made to die for others to shine as it was with Jesus and Moses. Life itself is for the survival of the fittest and the one with God, even if they walked through the valley of the shadow of death and were never left alone.

Besides that, connection with the cloud of darkness at night is also a formidable force to overcome for your brightness to illuminate.

Positioning is another factor that hinders most people from fulfilling their mandate to shine. It is not only about putting fire on your candle to bring light, but it is also paramount where the candle is placed. Some people will find purpose in life and will not fulfil purpose because they are in a different place and their star is in another place, and until they travel or migrate to connect with their star, they cannot shine no matter their efforts, prayers, educational attainment or social status. To provide light to everyone in the house, to continue to be born and remain relevant, you must be in a place where you get a continuous supply of air to keep their light burning.

All, most enemies do is separate you from the star by adopting fear, threats, intimidation, and frustration. Jesus was driven to Egypt just to allow his enemies to die. Then he had to return home to where the star was seen, where the star was sent, and where the star would shine, for the whole world would hear of it and come to the light of his shining.

"A light to lighten the Gentiles and the glory of the people of Israel." (Luke 2:2)

"The people which sat in darkness saw great light and to them which sat in region and shadow of death light is sprung up" (Matt 4:16)

These prove the importance of your location and the relation of your star to the time appointed by your creator for your star to shine for all to see.

"Ye are the light of the world. A city that is set on a hill cannot be hidden. Neither do men light a candle and put in under the bushel basket, but on the candle stick and it giveth light unto all that are in the house" (Matthew 5:14-15)

Remember that whatever you are given, you are given for others and benefit those around you. No matter what you do for a living, life is about how much you give to others. The light was illuminated for all in the house - your neighbours and wherever you were located at the time. You are blessed to be a blesser. No gift of God was given to man because of the man who got the gift but for the benefit of all around him.

If you are a hairdresser, do you start a salon to dress your hair? No, you use your gift, talent, or skill to serve others, and they, in turn, reward or compensate you by payment for services rendered. This is true of every profession and trade.

CHAPTER 2
WILDERNESS

Wilderness is a place of isolation, desolation, survival, preparation, training to rediscover yourself, and a place where your device means to sort yourself out all alone.

Passing through the wilderness of life can be a herculean task which requires doggedness, perseverance, endurance, tenacity, determination, ruggedness, and resilience to manoeuvre through bends, sand, wild plants, wild animals, mountains, and rivers. The race is like a marathon, where about fifty thousand start, but only 500 get to the finishing line.

The end of the marathon is better than the beginning because not everyone is destined to succeed, but we are all allowed to start the race and given the same amount of time each day. Thereby allowing afflictions, persecution, bullies, the beast in the wilderness and all other forces to the sheaving out the chaff from the wheat, only the strongest will survive.

"...And said, behold I have dreamed a dream more: and the eleven stars made obeisance to me" (Genesis 37:9)

Even the eleven brothers, too, had their stars but could not shine beyond their locality. As long as Joseph was with them, their stars could not shine because they needed to arise to be able to shine. Joseph's star was waiting for him in Egypt, and he needed adversaries, enemies, and adversities to drive him and push him away from where he was in his comfort zone to where his star was waiting. No normal circumstances could achieve this. He had to carry food to his ten brothers in the wilderness, and there he went and a conspiracy was hatched, and he went from one affliction to another.

"Behold, I have refined thee, but not with silver; I have chosen thee and the furnace of affliction" (Isaiah 48:10)

The rise of a young, inexperienced boy in his teens sold into slavery, taken in the chain and brought down to Egypt through the wilderness. He found himself among a strange culture, strange people, strange language and religion, but he quickly adjusted to life in his new environment without

grudges, and a bulk passing carried out, he discharged his daily duties joyfully, giving him multiple promotions in the foreign land.

In Egypt he connected with his star but went through the wilderness of rejection and betrayals until the appointed time came, when God troubled the king of Egypt, and Joseph was sought after.

His transformation from grass to glory took thirteen good years. But when the appointed time came, God made him relevant and prominent. A nonentity was given an identity, and he stood out and became outstanding.

"Behold, I send an Angel before thee, too keep thee in the way and to bring thee into the place which I have prepared" (Exodus 23:20)

Even for the Israelites to inherit their fortune of the land flowing with milk and honey, they had to have the wilderness experience.

"Who led thee through the great and terrible wilderness, wherein were fiery serpents and scorpions and drought, where there was no water; who brought thee forth water out the rock of flint. Who fed thee in the wilderness with manna, which thy fathers knew not, that he might humble thee, and he might prove thee to do thee good at thy latter end. And thou say in thine heart, My power and might of my hand hath gotten me this wealth. But thou shalt remember the LORD thy God: for it is he that giveth thee power to get wealth, that he may establish is covenant which he swore unto thy father, as it is this day." (Deuteronomy 8:15-18)

The wilderness is a terrible place, but all pathfinders, front runners, trailblazers, trendsetters, and groundbreakers must all be ready and willing to suffer affliction and rejection. No journey is fun. The world itself is not a bed of roses, and there are no wilderness journeys without wounds, bruises and scars to tell the story of the experience.

There, you meet the scorpions, the serpent, the bears, the lions, and the tigers, all looking for whom to devour. There, you experience draught, famine and all manners of unfavourable weather conditions, which you must adapt and adjust to survive. It is the most difficult pathway to navigate, and you will be humbled by the things you experience and the inhumane treatment you receive from people you meet in a very hard and harsh environment.

These teach us humility and tell us that all things are good and that if we eventually survive the trials and travails of the wilderness, he should be given the honour due to him.

Most of those who never go through wilderness training and preparation before manifestations will eventually lose what they have received because getting to the top of the ladder of the success of life is not as important as remaining there, at the top. So many forces who want what you have will not wish you well, and from experience, it becomes history if you cannot manage and maintain the position. King Saul got the kingship without due process, without sacrifice and without experience in human management, and he eventually failed. To whom much is given, much is expected is a biblical proverb of old.

"...For unto whomsoever much is given, of him shall be much required: and to whom men have committed much, of him they will ask the more." (Luke 12:48)

Ignorance is a tenable excuse in law, but the stupidity of the highest order and the leadership failure. Remember, those who preside over might be richer, wiser, bigger, taller, older, better and even more educated than you. If fortune has smiled on you and given you the advantage of the privilege over such class geniuses, watch your steps, utterances and actions because many are warming up from the reserve bench, ready to replace and displace you and bench you forever with their extraordinary performance. Don't take where you are and what you have for granted; they are the desires of those you rule and those behind you. It is the nature of man to take orders and directives from another man of lesser age, lesser education, and lesser talent and skills, but we are all resigned to fate and accept the circumstances in which we find ourselves. We cannot change; if we can, we will change it. King Saul missed the mark and fell short of God's and man's expectations of him.

However, some might argue about someone like King Solomon, who never experienced the wilderness of life; this is purely the result of ripping what his father, King David, planted and sacrificed to achieve. But Kish, the father of Saul, paid no price and gave no sacrifice to justify the position given on the platter of gold. If full payments are not made, the blessing is not secured and is not guaranteed to last. We all get trained to go through the furnace of affliction, which humbles us and allows the smith to shape us into whom he designed us to be.

The wilderness brings out the best in everyone and makes us good leaders and managers of human resources.

One of the simplest things in life is to be chosen, ordained, anointed, appointed, but how do you navigate yourself to the position without going through the wilderness for your training and preparation because the promised land or throne you aspire to acquire is not vacant, and you must be prepared to upstage the established structure on ground and the power in incumbency. The wilderness experience is not a punishment for sin or an experiment but a training and preparation ground to prepare us to face the task, assignment and challenges. David's choice was very easy, and he effortlessly got the anointing and approval of God and the prophet, but that was the beginning and end of a journey. The anointing caused him to be driven away from home, his natural habitat where he has lived all his life. And he wondered for a year from one wilderness to another in such a place of refuge, surviving only on raiding towns and villages to feed himself and the four hundred men who were within, whose number increased to six hundred.

Now, talking about four hundred men, these were not the people God anointed David to lead and rule over, but the throne was not vacant at that time, and despite their anointing, it would not get on the plate of gold.

These four hundred men, ordinary men in debt, failures in societies, and miscreants, remind me of when I was a youth and tailoring apprentice. No master gave me expensive fabrics or materials of their customer until I mastered the arts of cutting cement paper bags and showed me dexterity and ability to handle fabrics. We then graduated to the less expensive materials fund in the fashion industry.

"And everyone who was in distress, and every one that was in debt, and every one that was discontented, gathered themselves unto him; and he became a captain over them: and there were with him about four hundred men." (Samuel 22:2)

This proves that those who cannot manage failures cannot manage success, which is why success is not commonly accessible to everyone. Those who had not managed animals as shepherds in those days will eventually fail in human management in the days of the patriarchs. Wilderness is not a place of comfort despite your anointing, your prophetic declarations or coronation; it is a place of adaptation to hard lifestyles, a place of the survivor of the fittest, a place of betrayal, a place of continuous battle, abandonment, frustration, a place where you fight with beast in human skin, a place of rejection, a place among the thorns where many were torn apart, a place of bruises and wounds, a place of injustice and hatred which if you survive these odds you don't graduate to rule over what you went through and conquered, life is not fair they say. King David, at this period, fled to the high priest and prophet Samuel for solutions to the barrage of problems confronting him. He tried to find help and solace in Samuel, who anointed him, but no help was forthcoming in a place of isolation to get a solution on your own alone.

"And the child grew, and waxed strong in spirit, and was in the deserts till the day of his shewing unto Israel." (Luke 1:80)

The desert, or the wilderness as the case might be, is the place of desolation and isolation to harden, toughen and test your power of endurance, tolerance, self-control, discipline and sacrifices. Let your wilderness define your character and let character mould you to whom God wants you to be, a yielded vessel of honour.

Here, John ate what he found around him, slept in the cold at night, and survived the scorching heat of the day, the wild animals and the wilderness while awaiting his days of manifestations. Note also that for thirty years, not much was written or heard about Jesus until the spirit of God took him to the wilderness, where he was made to go without food for forty and forty nights. He was adequately equipped empowered and formally confirmed for the divine assignment. It must not be earlier than the appointed time lest you hit the rock, as in the case of Moses in Egypt when he killed an Egyptian in defence of an Israelite.

"And Jesus being full of the Holy Ghost returned from Jordan, and was led by the Spirit into the wilderness." (Luke 4:1)

Take your wilderness experience with joy, as it is the only path to the throne and to the land of milk and honey. You can't skip the process because it is what makes the product durable and beautiful.

Apostle Paul, through Timothy, charges us all to 'Endure hardship' and to 'Endure afflictions.'

Apostle Peter made it clear that this issue affects everyone; many who aspire to be great, not only Christians, go through similar problems in life.

"Beloved, think it not strange concerning the fiery trial which is to try you, as through some strange thing happened unto you." (Peter 4:12)

Moses, Jesus, Joseph, Daniel, David, John, and many others all endured their own crosses without complaining, blaming anyone, or looking for excuses to avoid the inevitable. They eventually prevailed, and their victory was lasting and permanent because they had paid their dues and sacrificed to get to where they were.

They paid for what they had and never cut corners to reach their desired haven. It might not be pleasant, easy or comfortable, as it has never been to anyone, yet it is part of glory and greatness. Therefore, learn endurance, perseverance and self-control; you are almost there. Are you tired and on the brink of giving up? Yes, so happened to those before you, but they learned to encourage themselves and angels in the form of men came to encourage them, too. Remember that even Jesus in the flesh was almost giving up, but help came his way to encourage him and not change the course of the project.

"And he was withdrawn from them about a stone's cast, kneeled down, and prayed. Saying, Father, if thou be willing, remove this cup from me; nevertheless, not my will, but thine, be done. And there appeared an angel unto him from heaven,

strengthening him. And being in agony he prayed more earnestly: and his sweat was as it were great drops of blood falling down to the ground." (Luke 22:41)

Watch out and pray ceaselessly because the wilderness has swallowed up many promising and upcoming stars, and we hear no more of them because they can't survive the heat, the pressure and the persecutions on their part. Some say if God ordains it, it should be easy, but remember it was not easy for those before you who were ordained and charged with the deliverance of their people, leading a race raising a new generation of great and wealthy people, some even paid the ultimate price of leadership with their lives. You either be strong and fight for yourself and those coming behind you, or you fall back and follow the old orders. If you can't beat them, you join them. If things change course, someone must dare to pay the price of belling the cat among the group of mice. You cannot continue to debate and talk about the problem, but someone must rise to the occasion and make a difference. God has never come down to help men and will not come for you either. He sent men to help men, and you are reading this book because the onus falls on you to end the old and start the new by creating a niche for yourself and your descendants.

Passing through the waters, fire, and furnace in the wilderness leaves us with scars to tell the story of our challenges, betrayals, disappointments, and brokenness, where we have been, what we have gone through, how far we have come, the war and battles fought, the stories of our victories, failures, defeats, and some battles, the story of our survivors, and the territories we conquered.

Now, what story do your scars tell? How many times have you trusted those who left you devastated, heartbroken and traumatised? Your promotion and elevation are the reward for the battle fought and won. In the battle of life, when you get wounded, someone has to come to your aid to lift you up, wash your wound, band-aid your wound and keep you safe, but if there is no one available, encourage yourself to live, than to be captured and enslaved forever. The choice is yours.

Whatever you don't pay the valued price for, you won't enjoy the full benefits of it. Jesus paid the price for his crown of glory, John paid before his manifestations despite their Angelic prophetic birth, and David was also pursued in the wilderness for years, living and feeding on raids until his appointed time. You deserve some accolades. Now, pay your dues before they are due. You cannot rise above your star.

CHAPTER 3
BATTLE LINE

> *"Many a time they have afflicted me from my youth: yet they have not prevailed against me. The plowers plowed on my back: they made their furrows long." Psalm 129:2-3.*

This was a bittersweet experience for King David of Israel, and you will discover that life itself is a tragicomedy, a script in which you are the main actor. No one cares or gives a damn about you until you are rated above them, lifted above and beyond them, recognised and elevated, and become more prominent and relevant than others. As long as you are a part of the others, you are free, but the moment anything tries to distinguish you or make you stand out of the group, you instantly become everyone's assault target to tarnish your image and your reputation and to get you furious and discouraged. Once you have been singled out for any reason, prepare for war even from members of your own family who feel outsmarted and feel you are inferior to them and are not willing to relinquish power or position which they thought rightfully should belong to them. At this point, envy will divide most of your closest allies and friends to become antagonists and foes seeking your downfall. Not many are willing and ready to submit to any other person. Respect comes from sheer responsibility because you have no choice but to respect those who are due, even when they are much younger or have lesser achievements than you. It is a duty to respect your superior irrespective of other factors that you might consider inferior to you. People do not actually respect the leader, but the offices they occupy, and that is why when most leaders leave their positions, they become isolated, frustrated and feel betrayed.

These problems did not start yesterday; it's been an age-long attitude of men not feeling good when others are appreciated, commended, or elevated above them.

"And in the process of time, it came to pass, that Cain brought of the fruit of the ground an offering unto the Lord. And Abel, he also brought of the firstlings of his flock and of the fat thereof. And the Lord had respect unto Abel and to his offering: But unto Cain and to his offering he had no respect. And Cain was very wroth, and his countenance fell. And the Lord said to Cain, why art thou wroth? And why is thy countenance fallen?

Gen 4:3-6

As the eldest and firstborn, Cain has this right of entitlement that he should always be considered first before his junior brother. Still, destiny and attitudes don't follow orders and protocols of age, colour, race, gender, etc., in fact, success has no colour, no age limitation, no gender bias and no religious or tribal rules to be obeyed and followed. It has only the culture and traditions of those who understand the language and principles of success. That is why it is possible to see an atheist who believes in no God still prospering because they abide and are guided by the rules and principles of success and thus are worthy of their rewards.

The bone of contention should not be between Cain and Abel. Cain should have channelled his grievances and displeasure instead of venting his anger on Abel, but because God is invincible, he chooses to vent his anger on the innocent boy he can see.

Apostle James sums it up in a better narrative when he wrote in his letter:

"From whence come wars and fightings among you? Come thee not hence, even of your lusts that war in your members. Ye lust and have not: Ye kill, and desire to have, and cannot obtain: Ye fight and war, yet ye have not, because ye ask not. Ye ask, and receive not, because ye ask amiss, that ye may consume it upon your lusts" James 4:1-3

When people don't get what they want, they resort to violence against those who were fortunate enough to receive it. This form of vengeful anger leads to the death of many innocent souls who were just victims of circumstances. In fact, my people have an adage that says the unending and un-explained battle of envy because none of the fighters will openly declare that he or she is angry with the other person because they are better off or angry because of the blessings they received or because they are approved and preferred ahead of them. It is a pain that lives deep within the heart of the person having the grudges. He feels the only way to heal himself of this hurt or perceived injustice and remain relevant is to eliminate, slander or pull down the perceived rival who innocently never noticed them as a threat as another sin of the elders goes; if I can't have it, I'll destroy it, and no one else gets it. It is better to waste it than for someone inferior to them to have it because of their unwillingness to submit and serve a lesser person.

Now, back to Cain, whose countenance fell because of God's favourable approach to the sacrifice of someone he considered a lesser or junior person to him, we must not fail to realise that for anyone offering to be accepted, the giver of the offering must first be accepted before his offerings can be accepted. You cannot bribe God; Abel, as a person, was considered a better person before God, with a better attitude and approach. Anyone who doesn't like you won't like your gift or value your efforts and sacrifices. It is not that God hated Cain, but his attitude towards God defines God's attitude towards him, which is clear in verse seven of the same chapter: "If thou do well, shall thou not be accepted?"

The same analysis was used by Apostle Peter in the hands of the Gentile Centurion named 'Cornelius' *"Then Peter opened his mouth, and said of a truth I perceive that God is no respecter of persons: but in every nation he that feareth him, and worketh righteousness is accepted with him" (Act 10:34-35)*

God is no respecter of persons, yet those who fear God and do the work of righteousness are accepted by him irrespective of their position in the family, society, or the committee of friends.

Not even their religion would be a consideration for God's favour when making vital decisions. Cain was wroth and could not explain the reason for his anger and hatred for his brother. Here, the battle line is drawn because envy leads to anger, anger leads to hatred, and hatred leads to destructive actions to eliminate, exterminate or frustrate the favoured one. "Why art thou wroth? And why is thy countenance fallen?" There was no response because "The heart is deceitful above all things and desperately wicked; who can know it?". He has mischievous plans to get revenge on his brother at all costs because of the events which wasn't the fault of the brother.

Always beware of people with negative energy around you, they will contribute nothing to your success and are never happy with your achievements. They have a plan, and cannot be appeased by anything. You must beware of such friends, boss or family members whom you noticed never celebrate your success nor clap when you win, no enemy can be more dangerous than such people around you.

Later, "Cain talked with Abel, his brother" What was an angry man discussing with his victim? Study the countenance of the people around you every time you win, lest they entrap you with their persuasive words that will lead to your destruction, as they will go the extra mile to engage the services of others in order to achieve their aims. Learn to say no to some advances and advice and reject offers or invitations from unsure sources if you want to live long and achieve your goal. God saw what Cain was planning but will not stop evil perpetrators from perpetrating evil, but he expects you to wise up and rise and be proactive and smart enough to decode their plans. Most times, people blame God for their own stupidity and ignorance, asking why God did not stop their detractors. It is your duty to defend yourself, protect yourself, and avoid the gatherings and association of those whose countenance you felt wasn't right with you. It is better that you offend them than for them to destroy you.

Another good example of family members who became bitter by just hearing the prophetic vision of their young teenage brother and not wanted to be subject to him devised a means of eliminating him *"Now Israel loved Joseph more than all his children, because he was the son of his old age: and he made him a coat of many colours. And when his brethren saw that their father loved him more than all his brethren, they hated him and could not speak peaceably unto him. And he said unto them, Hear, I pray you, this dream which I have dreamed: For, behold, we were binding sheaves in the field, and, lo, my sheaf arose, and also stood upright; and, behold, your sheaves stood round about, and made obeisance to my sheaf." (Gen 37:3-7)*

One of the greatest downfalls of many innocent budding stars was their unguided utterances because they are like children who could not discern or know the difference between haters and lovers. They often make friends and confide in enemies whom they perceive as friends, brothers and sisters, cousins, uncles, nephews, and lovers. For Cain, God's love, preference and acceptance for his brother was his downfall, and for Joseph, his father's open display of affection for him above the other ten children provoked jealousy and moved the brothers to anger. To add salt to injury, he was a dreamer who confided in people he held in high esteem and had confidence in them as siblings to guide his steps to achieve the enviable position ahead of him. He turned out to be the architect of his predicaments.

Though we might all agree that God brought his ultimate plans out of their wicked, mischievous plans, the fact remains that you and I can learn from him because not everyone who falls victim to such criminal-minded people will come out a survivor. "Shall thou indeed reign over us? Or shall thou indeed have dominion over us? And they hated him yet the more for his dreams and for his words."

No one is ready and willing to be subject to someone of lesser ability, capability, age, knowledge or wealth, but those who do subject themselves do so by resigning to fate. *"And when they saw him afar off, even before he came near unto them, they conspired against him to slay him, and they said one to another, 'Behold, this dreamer cometh.'"*

Remember, this man has gone from one wilderness to another, carrying on his shoulders the burden of feeding his ten brothers, who were unknowing to him were plotting his demise while he is tasked with getting food for them. Are you, too, running helter-skelter to provide and meet the needs of some people who are unhappy with your dreams, vision, and success? Do you realise how bitter and angry your success has made some people? Don't give them the knife and the opportunity to stab you to death.

Looking at their well-scripted narratives, you will know they had made up their minds to kill him and were only waiting for an opportunity, which has now presented itself. Stop walking, talking and bragging among your haters whom you call friends and family members. *"Come now therefore, and let us slay him, and cast him into some pit, and we will say, some evil beast had devoured him, AND WE SHALL SEE WHAT WILL BECOME OF HIS DREAMS."*

There are visions, dreams, and destiny killers who believe life is unfair to them and believe they deserve better than the Gods. They have decided to bully, intimidate, threaten, and frustrate the fortunate ones to submission. In life, winners don't play rough; only losers go for anything to destroy the winner, "If you miss the ball, don't miss the leg" It means if you miss the target, don't leave others to go ahead of you, hack them down, backslide, backbite, backstab, nobody goes anywhere as long as they don't lead. They have this destructive instinct and are not willing to negotiate.

This is another case study of a warrior, a king, and the head of a nation who became very envious of a young boy who not only delivered Israel but also saved the king and the army of Israel from disgrace and embarrassment. Envy is not a product of the bad attitude of the victims but of the disgust and lack of contentment of their predators.

"And it came to pass as they came, when David was returned from the slaughter of the Philistine, that the women came out of all cities of Israel, singing and dancing, to meet King Saul, with tabrets, with joy, and with instruments of music. And the women answered one another as they played, and said, Saul hath slain his thousands, and David his ten thousands. And Saul was very wroth, and the saying displeased him; and he said, They have ascribed unto David ten thousands, and to me they have ascribed but thousands: and what can he have more but the kingdom?" (1 Samuel 18:6-8)

Sometimes in life, from the people we expect praises and commendations, we get hatred and anger from which the source cannot be traced. Anyone fighting you without any cogent reason is only angry at your success and can't voice it out, and no matter how many peace meetings you call, they will never be at peace with you. All your offer of peace will be met with resentment and more anger and bitterness. They will never be at peace with you and never at peace around you neither will they be at peace with themselves. Your haters are never-dying enemies who will go all out and leave no stone unturned to give whatever is required just to destroy you. King Saul went as far as giving his daughters to David (not because he loved David) or appreciated his prowess in battle but out of envy that David might rise and become more acceptable and popular than himself; he was under the illusionary fear of losing the throne, the crown and relevance to a mere boy.

Once upon a time, there was an Indian myth about a very wealthy king who had a very beautiful princess, and many kings desired to have her as a wife. the king later devised a way of getting the right suitor to marry his daughter. He decided to invite all the village men and openly declared that he had a task for them, and whoever could pass the task would be the lucky husband of his daughter. The winner would take half of his wealth and would eventually succeed him as king, and he wanted a brave, bold and confident man who could fight and take risks to defend his only daughter and the village. The men congregated and were taken to the man's pet poolside, filled with crocodiles. They charged anyone who could swim across to the other side to win the competition and marry the princess. It is an undaunted task, and many were not prepared to die for the sake of marrying a woman. This brings to memory one of my quotes: "Those who live for nothing will eventually die for nothing". You must define what is worth dying for in life before you can excel in your chosen field. It was getting dark, and after hours of meditations, no man was ready and willing to risk crossing a crocodile-infested pool.

Suddenly, the unexpected happened, and a man was found in the pool manoeuvring, dodging and edging forward, avoiding the jaws of the hungry crocodiles who were deliberately stabbed overnight for this purpose. Sometimes, its head goes below the water, and the people assume it drowned and was dead as drops of blood could be seen on the surface of the water.

Finally, he emerged at the other end with wounds and bruises sustained from the scales and jaws of the hungry predators desperately hunting for food. Everyone was left baffled and confused by what they had just witnessed and wondered how he had survived the onslaught of these reptiles. Though he came out with injuries, he survived and won the prize, but the first word he uttered after this great feat was, "Who pushed me?"

So many times, we find ourselves in unplanned, unpalatable, and very precarious situations, and I can deduce that "people become brave when the only option left for them to survive is bravery." He had no choice; he had to use every means possible to avoid the reptile's jaws, his swimming desterity, his agility, his bravery, and everything he could summon together to avoid death, not just about the prize at stake.

It was later discovered one of his haters who wanted revenge on him pushed him "to his death", but things turned around, and the death wishes became wealth, but not without a scar to tell the story of his near-death escapade. Most great people became great after a push, a sack letter, a termination of appointment, a failure or a rejection. This pushes them out of their perceived comfort zone to rediscover themselves. We all need a push out of our comfort zones to bring out the best in us. We need to be challenged, and when others don't believe in us, we have a point to prove by taking up the challenges and turning them into opportunities. Sometimes, we have gone too far to turn back, or it is too late to give up; we have to devise means of survival.

The wife of Potiphar pushed Joseph from his comfort zone into prison through her mischievous attitude and manipulation of her husband; we must notice that she remains the same while the

Joseph she pushed only became a better version of himself. Don't be afraid of the sudden push, though you are not prepared for it; it could be a push to glory and honour. We must learn how to turn adversity to our advantage by using the hard times to bring out the heroes within us. Our setback should be a setup for greatness if we use it as a stepping stone to climb the ladder of success. Success is a product of failure; perfection is a product of mistakes, and light is a product of darkness. Difficulties are God-given opportunities to grow, develop and keep us moving no matter how slow or difficult the terrain. Don't be where you used to be or where those who doubted you left you behind, make advancement, make progress. Never feel defeated, rejected, stuck, weak, or tired; keep encouraging yourself and get strength from within yourself.

Hard times, bad times, and difficulties are not peculiar to a particular person, race, or language; they happen to everyone who wants to achieve greatness, become relevant, and make history. So don't allow negative vibes from negative people to cloud your sense of judgement, and never hold anyone around you responsible for your failure or your predicament; those who find excuses won't find solutions. They continue to give reasons why they are where they are. One of the toughest experiences encountered by many these days has forced many into suicide and depression, a job loss, and getting fired are things that can traumatise and frustrate a young man as he wonders 'where do I start from?' however many people came out of the 'fired' and survived to become billionaires because they never gave up on themselves. J.K. Rowling was a secretary of the London office of Amnesty International but was shown the way out, and she did use the sacking to fulfil her purpose of being a global writer. In 1919, Walt Disney was fired from the Kansas City Star because he was said to 'lack imagination and had no good ideas'. Today, Disney World speaks for itself. A Baltimore TV producer told Oprah Winfrey that she was 'unfit for television news'; today, she is a global icon in the broadcasting industry.

Thomas Edison was fired up by his teacher's comment that 'he was addled'. Let the 'fire' fire you up to greatness, not anger and bitterness.

The list is endless, and I would not like to bore you with the names of school dropouts who eventually became billionaires like Bill Gates, Mark Zuckerberg, Elon Musk, Steve Jobs, Richard Branson, and so many great men of virtue who used the opportunities they had to better their lot. Your present situation is not final until you make it your final destination; the choice is yours. Those who get bitter from the process experience will not improve with the product.

"Or what king, going to make war against another king, sitteth not down first, and consulteth whether he be able with ten thousand to meet him that cometh against him with twenty thousand? Or else, while the other is yet a great way off, he sendeth an ambassage, and desireth conditions of peace." (Luke 14:31-32)

In the battle of life, either spiritual or physical, we must first and foremost sit down to assess and quantify our strength, ability, capacity, and capability against the invading army. The first thing is consultation, and if we are found wanting or inadequately equipped against the opposition, we must settle for negotiation instead of going into battle. Secondly, we must know the accurate figures, strength and weapons possessed by the opposition before we proceed to fight in battle; once that is done, we have to get our defensive and offensive weapons ready for battle.

Now, let's sit down for stock-taking and evaluation before making a fool of ourselves and putting the lives of innocent people in danger. At this point, many would surrender after seeing or hearing about the enemy's might, prowess, achievements and the territories they've conquered, 'I can't come and kill myself' is their popular slang. They give up the pursuit of their dreams just like the majority of the Israelites who were focussed on the strength, the height and the looks of the enemies rather than focus on God's words and ability backed by his precedents. He who is afraid of death, will never inherit his father's throne, according to a popular adage.

To challenge the status quo, you must be very brave and bold, putting on the whole armour of God, which has both the defensive and the offensive weapons. Having come to the knowledge of who the enemies are, the awareness must help you to know the type of weapons to employ in combat against such fierce principalities, powers, rulers of the darkness of this age and spiritual hosts of wickedness in heavenly places.

The girdle is for your waist; no loose garments must be worn in battle. You have to be properly and smartly dressed to engage the enemies; you have to put on your breastplate to ensure your vital body organs (like your heart), which will be the primary aim of the enemies, are well protected from the enemies' arrows. Then, you have to shod your feet with boots that can withstand harsh and unfavourable weather conditions and aid you in movement and flight if needed.

Next, take up the shield to cover and block all the enemies' arrows, spears, and swords and ensure all parts of the body are adequately cared for and protected. This will help you put out and quench all the enemies' fiery darts.

Furthermore, one of your defensive weapons is your helmet, which is to cover and protect your skull and prevent you from the mental and emotional damage that can traumatise your life and rob you of mental sanity and soundness of mind, which is needed to adequately plan and win your battle.

You can see from the above that every soldier in battle is more defensive than offensive because safety first is a rule of life because once life is gone, every dream ends. The only known effective offensive weapon for all Christians is the sword of the spirit; every other thing works under the authority of the word.

Finally, the battle is won and lost in the mind before it actually begins, so your present achievement is a product of your mindset yesteryears.

CHAPTER 4
HAEMORRHAGE

In the battle of life, people silently nursed and bore all forms of injuries, pain, wounds, bruises and cuts in their flesh, which leave a scar after healing, and these scars tell the story of their survivors in the harsh, unfriendly terrain of the world. Whenever we get pierced, get a cut or get wounded, we all bleed as a result of the pain unleashed on us by life's situations and circumstances, but somehow, we survived the very hard blows that have claimed the lives of many and left many more as casualties bedridden.

As survivors in the battle of life, you must have been involved directly or indirectly in the battle of survival, progress or something worth fighting for, and as my saying goes, 'anything not worth dying for is not worth fighting for, and anything not worth fighting for is not worth dying for'. Since we all will eventually die one day, then we should live and fight to get whatever we desire to acquire because no one will give you – even what belongs to you – on a platter of gold even if it is your right. The world is a place for fighters, even in the animal kingdom; it is a place where survival is the right of the fittest, those who can run and hunt at the same time. You must be brave and bold enough to confront the challenges and strong enough to challenge every authority that withstood your progress. *"And Rachel said, With great wrestlings have I wrestled with my sister, and I have prevailed: and she called his name Naphtali." (Genesis 30:8)*

Jacob, too, was not just satisfied with prophecies, visions and dreams; he did not become complacent as he had had more than enough promises; he needed to fight and fought for what he wanted, and because of it, his sheer determination he was not disappointed, he tactically dispatched his wives, children, servants and herds to remain alone and to fight for his dear life in the wilderness in order to redefine and rediscover his destiny, it is a lone battle, you are on your own.

"And Jacob was left alone; and there wrestled a man with him until the breaking of the day. And when he saw that he prevailed not against him, he touched the hollow of his thigh; and the hollow of Jacob's thigh was out of joint, as he wrestled with him. And he said, Let me go, for the day breaketh. And he said, I will not let thee go, except thou bless me. And he said unto him, What is thy name? And he said, Jacob. And he said, Thy name shall be called no more Jacob, but Israel: for as a prince hast thou power with God and with men, and hast prevailed." (Gen 32:24-28)

This battle is not just about a name change but a destiny-changing encounter that changed the course of his life and redefined his purpose as a covenant child. However, everything came at a price as the hollow of Jacob's thigh became disjointed and dislocated, which he lived with for the rest of his life. Because he is a generational destiny pioneer, his descendants were barred from eating the sinew that shrank in any meat. "He halted upon his thigh" This is the wound which led to his partial disability until his death. Most of the time, on the battlefield, we are tired and feel like giving up. We might be down, but fortunately, we are not counted out yet; aluta continua is our slogan for never giving up on anything thrown at us on the battlefield. *"Reproach hath broken my heart; and I am full of heaviness: and I looked for some to take pity, but there was none; and for comforters, but I found none." (Psalm 69:20)*

Weeping or crying for every full-grown adult who is not being beaten or going through any physical assault is a form of bleeding because of the trauma, the pain, the mental and the emotional torture, the depression, the betrayal, the disappointment, and the frustrations that accompany life's daily routine are too numerous to be counted but yet we survived against all odds *"Yea, he had power over the angel, and prevailed: he wept, and made supplication unto him: he found him in Bethel, and there he spake with us;" (Psalm 69:20)*

Reproach is a heartbreaker, and once one's heart is broken, nothing follows, but profuse bleeding of tears, sorrow and blood are the regular trademarks left behind on the victims. Nobody gives attention to a nobody. Pick yourself from the dust, dust yourself up and bind up your wounds, and learn to encourage yourself if no one else does, with no self-pity, regrets, or self-condemnations. He who wants to eat the honey stored in the belly of the rock should not spend precious time pitying or looking at how damaged and crushed the axe teeth are. People celebrate success and not strugglers whose efforts have not yet paid off. The bitter truth is your preparedness for any eventuality is paramount, as you will be treated cruelly and badly without pity, even when and where you deserve one.

You cannot change the course of history or be the forerunner for your generation when you don't want to risk your life by fighting against beasts in human form and ready to take the bull by the horns; only those who dare to be different can achieve greatness and glory for themselves and those coming after them.

"Many bulls have compassed me: strong bulls of Bashan have beset me round. They gaped upon me with their mouths, as a ravening and a roaring lion. I am poured out like water, and all my bones are out of joint: my heart is like wax; it is melted in the midst of my bowels. My strength is dried up like a potsherd; and my tongue cleaveth to my jaws; and thou hast brought me into the dust of death. For dogs have compassed me: the assembly of the wicked have inclosed me: they pierced my hands and my feet. I may tell all my bones: they look and stare upon me." (Psalm 22:12-17)

The piercing, the wounds, the agony, the pain, the rejections, the dejections, and the bleeding are all part of the glory story. Unease lies in the head that wears the crown, but even before the crown of glory comes the crown of story, which is thorny, and only the brave and strong men can survive it.

"...And they shall look upon me whom they have pierced, and they shall mourn for him, as one mourneth for his only son, and it shall be in bitterness for him, as one that is in bitterness for his firstborn" (Zechariah 12:10)

As the victims of such bitterness, you must have revenge in your mind but surrender all to God as you fight on for the crown of glory. There is no great man in the world who became a warrior without fighting a battle, a champion without competition, a leader without a group to lead, a king without a kingdom and none of them can succeed without a scar from the battles they fought and won. There is no overnight success but gradual graduation from grass to grace; that is the way God's prosperity works.

We must all go through one furnace of affliction or the other to refine, purify, redefine and get rid of dross and impurities living behind pain and the scars to linger on.

"Behold, I have refined thee, but not with silver; I have chosen thee in the furnace of affliction." (Isaiah 48:10)

We were specially selected and elected as peculiar people to pass through the refiner furnace to bring out the best in every one of us. After all, hindrances have been removed, like pride, selfishness, worldliness, etc., we then come out of the furnace better, purer, and greater than we ever thought we could, but we have to endure the smith hammers for proper shaping into what design he has in mind to fashion out of everyone. Being righteous does not save us from the refiner's furnace, nor does holiness give us immunity against the smith hammers and the smelting furnace because, without that, we will never be what his original design for each person is.

"Many are the afflictions of the righteous: but the Lord delivereth him out of them all." (Psalm 34:19)

The only assurance we've been given is that of ultimate victory and deliverance out of the furnace at God's appointed time. Some of us are as hard and strong as diamonds; some are gold and silver. Some others are steel or iron, but they are all malleable and have various melting points and levels of tolerance and endurance of pain. It is worth knowing that some other metals are aluminium and wood, which cannot endure the heat of the fire but get destroyed.

No matter how strong we may be, every metal has a melting point, and everyone has values placed on them, but we find solace and consolation in our God that he will always find a way to escape from every trouble before we reach our melting point.

"...there was given to me a thorn in the flesh, the messanger of satan to buffet me, lest I should be exhalted above measure" (2 Corinthians 12:7)

For a buffet means a sumptuous meal to be devoured, a meal to feed on, a blow to your jugular, to demobilise or paralyse your advancement. Life is never a bed of roses. For those who lived and changed the course of history or changed the course of their families to rely on, they had no choice but to get wounded among the thorns in the process of time.

"Then David and the people that were with him lifted up their voice and wept, until they had no more power to weep." (1 Samuel 30:4)

Despite the anointed and the prophecies, all protocols must be observed, and the ultimate price for stardom and glory must be paid. There's no shortcut for a man after God's heart like David to escape the torture and afflictions of his adversaries.

The Bible is filled with teary eyes from teary experiences of good and godly men who were not spared the agony and pain when subjected to one. Weeping comes before reaping because those who were subjected to pain and endured the pain will enjoy the gain.

"I am weary with my groaning; all the night make I my bed to swim; I water my couch with my tears. Mine eye is consumed because of grief; it waxeth old because of all mine enemies." (Psalm 6:6-7)

This shows the pain we go through daily in our various closets, unknown to the people we rule, lead, and govern. We hide away our tears from people who look up to us for strength, encouragement, and inspiration; they must not see us in our brokenness lest they, too, lose hope in the success project. We are grieved daily, but we keep displaying bravery as we wear laughter to the outside world while we die daily inwardly and still keep all hopes alive.

To make things worse for some of us who spend time tarrying and awaiting the manifestations of God in our situations, the enemies taunt us, mock us and reproach us, asking us to face where the God that has kept us waiting as we keep waiting and suffering in expectations.

"My tears have been my meat day and night, while they continually say unto me, Where is thy God?" (Psalm 42:3)

Making a mockery of your faith is not peculiar to you alone. Many great men have gone through the same route and come back with testimonies because he who promised is faithful and cannot fail even if he tarries; we were encouraged to wait for him.

Weeping is synonymous with bleeding to most adults who are going through the furnace of affliction.

"Surely he hath borne our griefs and carried our sorrows: yet we did esteem him stricken, smitten of God, and afflicted. But he was wounded for our transgressions; he was bruised for our iniquities: the chastisement of our peace was upon him, and with his stripes, we are healed." (Isaiah 53:4-5)

Who then is free if Jesus our Lord was allowed to be beaten, smitten, to be grieved, to be assaulted, to be insulted, to be molested, abused, accursed, stricken, abhorred, rejected, betrayed, abandoned, forsaken, afflicted and persecuted by mobs and eventually bled to death shamefully with a crown of thorns and blood oozing out of his head, hands, heart and feet. God's love will not spare you, too, but prepare you for the show of brutality you have to endure before you rule over your captors.

"But one of the soldiers with a spear pierced his side, and forthwith came there out blood and water." (John 19:34)

Without this bleeding, Jesus wouldn't be the mediator of a new covenant and no remission of sin to humanity. All things happen for a reason and under the permissive will of God, and some other things are for a season; these too shall pass, and your tears and bleeding will heal, leaving the scars that never heal to tell the story of the bitter experiences you have been through. However, there are numerous wounds in the hearts of men that no one sees; it is called internal injuries, which cause internal bleeding. For these injuries, no doctor has the power to heal; it is easy when people bleed out; we can bind the wound by the application of alcohol and oil for treatment, but for internal bleeding or a broken heart, no counsellor, no doctor and no psychologist has the antidote for the cure.

But in the book of Prophet Isaiah, the anointing he said to be equipped to heal the brokenness of every heart.

"...to bind up the brokenhearted" (Isaiah 61:1)

The anointing of God is the only medication that can gain access into the innermost part of a man's heart, which no doctor or medication can access but still leaves behind for everyone healed from a broken heart due to betrayal, being jilted and being rejected, a scar to tell the story.

There is life in our blood; every time we bleed, we give up a part of us to get part of his and be refreshed and renewed in our mortal bodies. Are you bleeding? By the anointing, you are healed.

CHAPTER 5
THORN IN THE FLESH

"There was given me a thorn in my flesh, the messenger of Satan to buffet me."

The irony of this statement is that as God by his Spirit uses men to facilitate and achieve his mission, so does the devil called Satan use men to haunt other men, to victimise them, to terrorise them, to threaten them and wear them out and probably tear them down until it prevails.

"...and shall wear out the saints of the Most High" (Daniel 7:25)

They can come in dreams, visions and in various other forms of manifestations to frighten the hell out of you so that you can continue to fast nonstop and to pray just to punish and wear you out of your strength until your faith is weakened when results are not commensurate with efforts.

"And her adversary also provoked her sore, for to make her fret..." (1 Samuel 1:6)

These people hunt down their victims and make their lives bitter and broken, making them feel inferior, inadequate, empty, desolate, barren, unproductive, unworthy and worthless. This grief of the heart makes the heart heavy and in need of a place to pour out their pain and be relieved of the burden that plagues the heart, whose wound is only known and seen by the victim. From this state of bitterness and grief, Hannah went to the presence of the Lord because the husband's approach to solving her problem was to give her more and more meat, which would not heal a wounded soul of her bitterness. Who is provoking you to anger, frustration and bitterness? They have done the same for people before you and will gladly do the same for you.

Hannah was enjoying a special favour of love from her husband, better than Peninnah. Hence, she became a victim and was driven crazy by her rival's attitude to taunt her and make a mockery of her state of barrenness. In fact, she made it a point of duty to constantly remind her of her weakness, her failure, her inability and her state of barrenness; this made Peninnah happy, fulfilled and excited, getting at her opponent at every opportunity, which in turn made Hannah constantly unhappy and couldn't even recognise nor appreciate the efforts and love of her husband which could not take away her reproach and shame.

At their prime, some people want to cut others to size, like those they see as a threat, those who have what they don't have, or those who have honed what they think should be theirs. Young trees are managed, pruned, and cut to size to control them and allow them to grow in a particular pattern or direction before they harden and mature. The same goes for humans: catch them young, rule them, or ruin them.

When you succeed where they failed, when you are a carrier of potential and are loaded or when you are gifted and often get special treatment than others, when you get the accolades, when they get intimidated by your success, just take note that nobody hunts down an empty barrel. The fact that you are a victim shows how much value is being placed on you and how much sacrifice they were also willing to risk just to get you down at all costs. That goes a long way to show your importance, despite the fact you see yourself as someone still struggling for survival but they have seen your stars and are not ready or willing to serve under you, and the only way to prevent that and to curb your progress is to come for you.

For years, King Saul went from one trick to another, chased David to every hole in the wilderness from every town to village and hunted him day and night to get rid of him. So governance became a part-time duty to King Saul as his priority shifted from his primary duty to search for his small, potentially gifted boy in his kingdom. He said, "Bring him up to me in bed, that I may slay him."

He further accused his son Jonathan of betrayal and sought to kill his son for not being an accomplice in the search for David and his eventual elimination as he reiterated: "For as long as the son of Jesse liveth upon the ground, thou shall not be established..." (1 Samuel 20:31)

However, it should be noted that Jonathan has accepted and agreed to the inevitable and has aligned himself with David as a subordinate. Still, his father, King Saul, won't accept such a deal, which belittles his office and the power of incumbency.

"...Fear not: for the hand of Saul my father shall not find thee: and thou shall be King over Israel, and I shall be next unto thee and that also Saul my father knoweth" (1 Samuel 23:17)

It is one thing to know, and it is another thing to accept the obvious and the inevitable. King Saul saw it coming but could not accept nor condone such an arrangement that wouldn't favour his immediate family. That's why some of us have no rest as we are daily pursued and hunted to bring us down and stop us from achieving set goals.

The word of God admonishes us to look unto Jesus as our example of endurance under pressure and persevere under persecutions and tribulations.

"Looking unto Jesus the author and finisher of our faith; who for the joy that was set before him endured the cross, despising the shame..." (Hebrews 12:2)

The key word above is endurance for everyone who chooses to rise and shine even amid the thorns piercing and tearing our skin and flesh apart; there's no shortcut to glory; if they come for Jesus, they will equally come for you. For every legacy there must be story of enduring and persistent fighters who choose to go through the pain to rewrite the storyline.

"...in labours more abundant, in stripes above measure, in prisons more frequent, in deaths oft. Of the Jews five times received I forty stripes save one. Thrice was I beaten with rods, once was I stoned, thrice I suffered shipwreck, a night and a day I have been in the deep; In journeyings often, in perils of waters, in perils of robbers, in perils by

mine own countrymen, in perils by the heathen, in perils in the city, in perils in the wilderness, in perils in the sea, in perils among false brethren; In weariness and painfulness, in watchings often, in hunger and thirst, in fastings often, in cold and nakedness." (2 Corinthians 11:23-27)

Please, what can be more traumatic and depressing than the above experience of a man seen as a saint and a righteous man who has chosen the path angels dare not tread, a path of honour and glory yet was not spared the troubles from the oppositions? These patriarchs all learned to be patient in tribulations and held on to their dreams, visions and prophecies without wavering in the midst of turbulence. They do not compromise but conform to the standard set before them by God. They refuse to negotiate away their freedom nor agree to give up on their dreams to preserve their lives.

Apostle Paul was not bragging when he gave an account of his experiences and encounters, such as how he fought and won against beasts of Ephesus who opposed his mission and commission and threatened to kill him. That is why he further charges the Philippians;

"And in nothing terrified by your adversaries: which is to them an evident token of perdition..." (Philippians 1:28)

Therefore, we find consolation in the word of God and comfort through the spirit of the living God which keeps our hopes alive and keeps assuring us of a better end for the Bible says, *"For I know the thoughts that I think toward you, saith the LORD, thoughts of peace and not of evil, to give you an expected end" (Jeremiah 29:11)*

The end always justifies the means or the investment, as he who laughs last always laughs best. It is not time to rest on your oars; keep the sail afloat and keep looking unto the hills that have provided all the needed help for those who pass through the same thorns thousands of years before you. Learn from them and get wisdom. If you are going on a smooth and straight road unchallenged or without any uprising and opposition or resistance, you might either be going downward or travelling in the wrong direction; that is when no one will be interested in you because the end of such a journey brings no success and achievement. But when you embark on a journey, and there seems to be an alarm that suddenly wakes everyone up and sets them against you, it means you are doing what is right and going in the right direction. Many times, the sea current has hijacked the movement of the boats and carried them to a different direction from their set shore. It must be a battle of wits to get things going right again; you must struggle with the wind against the storm and against the current driving the boats astray. The oppositions are the only proof to show you that you are developing, growing, advancing, and progressing in the right direction. You are doomed if no one comes for you; nothing will be achieved without opposition.

"And some fell among thorns; and the thorns sprung up and choked them." (Matthew 13:7)

"He also that received seed among the thorns is he that heareth the word; and the care of this world, and the deceitfulness of riches, choke the word, and he becometh unfruitful. (Matthew 13:22)

Falling among the thorns can be a devastating experience as they grow faster than the seed, and their main assignment is to choke and snuff life out of every seed that falls among them. They are also those who are anxious and worried about so many things and cannot achieve anything because the deceitfulness of riches diverted them from their set goals, and their lives became unfruitful.

When you are hurt, you bleed and shed tears of disappointment; count it all joy because a butterfly with all its beautiful and glamourous colour will always be torn among the thorns; that means there are no go areas for people with potential and careers of glory. No one before you in this body of flesh has ever survived the thorns without being torn apart left with laceration, scarification or injuries, which they will continue to nurse after that.

When Jesus was about to die, he lamented that the spirit was willing to drink the cup, but the flesh was weak. He then solicited the prayers of three of his devotees whom he had hardly taught how to pray before then; suddenly, in times of distress, he expected them to be instant prayer warriors, which were alien to them. These people had never prayed alone for ten minutes and were suddenly tasked with continuous prayer for sixty minutes. It was a defining moment for Christ, as powerful as he is, despite the anointing. Human weaknesses are exposed in his moment of trials and tribulations.

"Who in the days of his flesh, when he had offered up prayers and supplications with strong crying and tears unto him that was able to save him from death, and was heard in that he feared;" (Hebrews 5:7)

This shows that all humans are subject to one form of weakness or another. He prayed he lamented, he made supplications, he cried and wept, calling for help to save him from the moment and season of embarrassment, but no help came his way; the only help that came was those of angels that came to encourage and strengthen him to endure and finish his race and drink the cup set before him. That is precisely what I'm doing to you, to comfort you in battle, to encourage and strengthen you, to believe in God and in yourself, to let you know that your present problem is not peculiar to you alone or because of your sin or the sins of your ancestors, it is the path and the route to greatness and for God to be glorified.

"And there appeared an angel unto him from heaven, strengthening him. And being in an agony he prayed more earnestly: and his sweat was as it were great drops of blood falling down to the ground." (Luke 22:43-44)

If Christ could ask for help in such a dire season of trial and persecution, who are you not to call for help when you are in a dilemma? We all need someone who believes in us, sees our potential, encourages us, and motivates us not to give up when we feel like giving up when we are tired and weary on the way. Do not be proud to ask for help, do not be ashamed to ask for help and do not let overconfidence deny you the much-needed support.

"Comfort ye, my people," says God through Prophet Isaiah, and Jesus also left with the promise of a comforter after what he experienced; he knew we all needed help not to skip the test but to pass the exam and to overcome every form of the affliction we are thrown into.

CHAPTER 6
AUDACITY OF FAITH

Some projects are solely for the audacious in character, those who are bold, courageous, ambitious, daring, confident, arrogant, and those who disregard protocols, personal safety or the conventional ways of doing things. They are those who are ready and willing to take up the challenges headlong with the "If I die, I die" attitude of Queen Esther to achieve a set goal. They do not care about their lives or the criticisms of their critics, but this spurred them on to greater heights. They always think outside the box; they're not guided by rules but by vision; they go the extra mile and do extraordinary things to fight against all oppositions, tyrants, oppressions, repressions, and those they perceive will threaten their way of achieving purpose.

I have numerous living examples of such men with the boldness and the effrontery to take the bull by the horns and call a bluff of anyone who doubted their ability to succeed; they prove doubters wrong, they survived rejections, failures, self-disappointment, self-guilt, self-condemnations, depressions and frustrations and found their feet again after every fall, no wonder it is said "the downfall of a man is not the end of his life".

Your present state of predicaments is not final until you make it final, but remember that those who give up don't get up; they just adjust to life on the ground where they found themselves after they fell, living on crumbs for survival instead of rising after every fall. God ordained hard times to make people strong, bring out the best in them, and give them the revelation of the solutions around them. When planet Earth was created, it was created with all the necessary raw materials needed for a good and comfortable life; these materials today are employed in the manufacturing of our cars, our gadgets, our automobiles, our buildings and other materials used in our days, despite the fact that all these raw materials were buried under the belly of the earth like gold, diamond, silver, iron, magnesium, aluminium, titanium and even uranium used for atomic bombs etc. There was no time God told Adam or man what was buried in the belly of the earth; man was left in the harsh cold and hot weather naked to fashion out a way of survival, comfort and pleasure. The man was never told or instructed on how to get salt for his food, never taught how to get fire to cook his food, and was made a farmer but never taught how to make farming implements; hard times, challenges, necessity and adversity taught man to search the belly of the earth and all around him to discover all these metals for the use of humanity, there's no shortcut, God wants us to learn by what we suffered, man was told to replenish the earth, subdue the earth and have dominion over everything upon the earth. So, the onus falls on man to discover everything within the earth to make his sojourn pleasurable, but not the task of God to teach anybody where and how to get these things. Suffering, afflictions and challenges taught man the greatest lessons of life.

"Though he were a Son, yet learned he obedience by the things which he suffered;" (Hebrews 5:8)

Even Christ Jesus was not made perfect until he learnt obedience to natural laws that governs all humans and the law of life and death. He was humbled by what he suffered and became better thereafter.

The human project took probably millions or thousands of years of pain, hardship, failure, mistakes, and exposure to unfavourable weather conditions and natural disasters to get to where we are today, where we can choose types of cars to ride, types of houses to live in, types of furniture, types of electronic gadgets, even to designer shoes and dresses, these all took time to accomplish. How does man learn the edible plants and the ones that could kill? It is all by trial and error, which inevitably costs some people their lives; the trial and error and the mistakes have now led to great manufacturing feats and the production of so many weapons, instruments and equipment for the betterment of humanity.

Back to the story of our audacious man of valour who turned around his situations, made a success of his failures and frustrated the tokens of his critics.

"And the children struggled together within her; and she said, If it be so, why am I thus? And she went to enquire of the Lord. And the Lord said unto her, Two nations are in thy womb, and two manner of people shall be separated from thy bowels; and the one people shall be stronger than the other people; and the elder shall serve the younger." (Genesis 25:22-23)

"And after that came his brother out, and his hand took hold on Esau's heel; and his name was called Jacob: and Isaac was threescore years old when she bare them." Genesis 25:26)

The battle and the struggle to excel in life did not start today; it is a long battle from conception through the ages of life unto death. Man must not stop learning, growing and developing. If he does, he will be left behind in the grand scheme of things. The children struggled even before knowing good from bad. Man is indeed born for troubles but has to learn to turn those troubles and struggles into success by the domination of his domain. Here, one of the twins is said to be stronger than the other as they struggle in the womb of their mum. One was a weakling that would be subdued and forced to serve the stronger. Survival is for the fittest and the strongest; man has always ruled over man, and man has often taken advantage of other men whenever they are smarter, stronger, knowledgeable. One of the two strugglers was named Jacob, a supplanter, a con man, a cheat, who was always holding and pulling back the heels of his brother, who was going ahead of him at birth, aluta continua, the second was named Esau. It was a hunter who was loved more by the father who often eat of his game and the other a man dwelling in a tent 'mummy's boy' tied to mummy's apron, always around the mother, never goes far away from home and more loved by her.

With the passage of time, the father was to release the family blessing on one of the two, and Daddy's favourite boy was chosen by the customs and traditions governing the position of the firstborn. He was then charged to go hunting and cook for the father the delicacies he has often brought to him, but this time, it must be a special, sumptuous meal which was required for the release of the blessings; it had to be fresh meat, newly prepared, not what they had at home. However, the mother outsmarted him when she overheard the requests of the father to the senior son; she then encouraged the junior brother (who is always at home with her) after the senior had gone hunting for venison to act swiftly before the brother could find any venison to cook. The tricks worked as the senior brother took long to return; she took one of his hunting garments at home with her in her custody and gave it to the junior brother, took one of the flocks and quickly prepared it to be presented to the father for the junior to receive the blessings.

"And his mother said unto him, Upon me be thy curse, my son: only obey my voice, and go fetch me them. And he went, and fetched, and brought them to his mother: and his mother made savoury meat, such as his father loved. And Rebekah took goodly raiment of her eldest son Esau, which were with her in the house, and put them upon Jacob, her younger son: And she put the skins of the kids of the goats upon his hands, and upon the smooth of his neck: And she gave the savoury meat and the bread, which she had prepared, into the hand of her son Jacob." (Genesis 27:13-17)

The father, however, suspected foul play, but the script was well rehearsed and properly executed by the mother and the junior brother; this wasn't the first time that Esau has fallen for the mischief of Jacob as Jacob cunningly negotiated and bought over to himself the much-coveted birthright of the firstborn. Once beaten, twice shy, they said, but this was twice beaten.

"And he also had made savoury meat and brought it unto his father, and said unto his father, Let my father arise, and eat of his son's venison, that thy soul may bless me. And Isaac his father said unto him, Who art thou? And he said I am thy son, thy firstborn Esau. And Isaac trembled very exceedingly and said, Who? Where is he that hath taken venison, and brought it me, and I have eaten of all before thou comest, and have blessed him? yea, and he shall be blessed. And when Esau heard his father's words, he cried with a great and exceeding bitter cry, and said unto his father, Bless me, even me also, O my father. And he said, Thy brother came with subtlety and hath taken away thy blessing. And he said, Is not he rightly named Jacob? for he hath supplanted me these two times: he took away my birthright; and, behold, now he hath taken away my blessing. And he said Hast thou not reserved a blessing for me? And Isaac answered and said unto Esau, Behold, I have made him thy lord, and all his brethren have I given to him for servants, and with corn and wine have I sustained him: and what shall I do now unto thee,

my son? And Esau said unto his father, Hast thou but one blessing, my father? bless me, even me, and O my father. And Esau lifted up his voice and wept. And Isaac his father answered and said unto him, Behold, thy dwelling shall be the fatness of the earth, and of the dew of heaven from above; And by thy sword shalt thou live, and shalt serve thy brother; and it shall come to pass when thou shalt have the dominion, that thou shalt break his yoke from off thy neck." (Genesis 27:31-40)

This was the last straw that broke the camel's back; he was beaten hands down without remedy, he was betrayed by the very mother who gave him life, he was stripped of glory, honour and reputation, and he is no longer the first son and lost the right of a double portion of the inheritance. Now he has also lost the family ancestral blessings handed down from Abraham to Isaac, all is lost, he became devastated, a wounded lion, a hopeless and a hapless man, lost directions and lacked affections, he was disgruntled and desperate for revenge, he planned his revenge mission thinking he would recover back everything once the 'thief' that robbed him of all his inheritance died.

"And Esau hated Jacob because of the blessing wherewith his father blessed him: and Esau said in his heart, The days of mourning for my father are at hand; then will I slay my brother Jacob. And these words of Esau her elder son were told to Rebekah: and she sent and called Jacob her younger son, and said unto him, Behold, thy brother Esau, as touching thee, doth comfort himself, purposing to kill thee." (Genesis 27:41-42)

"And tarry with him a few days, until thy brother's fury turn away; Until thy brother's anger turn away from thee, and he forget that which thou hast done to him: then I will send, and fetch thee from thence: why should I be deprived also of you both in one day?" (Genesis 27:44-45)

The plan was hatched and awaiting execution, but the appropriate time of execution had not come; he waited as he wanted the father to die first before he could strike this. The mother overheard and devised a plan to send Jacob out of the city until the brother's anger and fury dissipated.

Now, when Esau saw that his brother Jacob was sent away, he sat down and rethought his resentment, anger, bitterness, and hatred against his brother and shelved his evil plans. The culprit is now on the run. He was left to rule his loss, bite his fingers, count his losses, and lick his wounds because he had shot himself in the foot. He then fashioned a new way to put an end to his frustration.

Suddenly, a plan struck his mind as he remembered the phrases from his father's words, "and by thy sword shall thou live" and "It shall come to pass when thou shall have the dominion that thou shall break his yolk from off thy neck". Eureka, eureka, I have found it as he repeated the words of Archimedes

"Then went Esau unto Ishmael, and took unto the wives which he had Mahalath the daughter of Ishmael Abraham's son, the sister of Nebajoth, to be his wife." (Genesis 28:9)

His first assignment was the task of overcoming anger and unforgiveness and his revenge mission; he then formed an ally by marriage with the Ishmaelites, who were good and raw hunters with fierce looks and great wealth of wilderness experiences, henceforth the Bible was silent on the journey of Esau as he struggled for survival, many will have thought his dreams and visions has ended because of his loss to his brother and many saw him as a never-do-well doomed and gone into oblivion, to some others he was a failure not worth talking about, a dullard and a big for nothing nincompoop.

Though nobody gave him a chance, this was a man at the height of the greatest betrayal by his mother, defrauded by his blood brother, and left hopeless by his father to roam and fend for himself for survival. It appears that even God was not interested in or well disposed of him; his dreams were shattered, scattered, and battered. He stumbled, fumbled several times, and eventually overcame against all odds to achieve what. No man believed he could achieve. He left home, left his people, left his family, left his land and left behind his anger and bitterness as he went in search of a new beginning. So he went, he saw, and he conquered; he has the nerve, temerity and dexterity to excel in his chosen field of hunting, and eventually became a warrior in battle. As time went on, he acquired slaves, workers, servants, herdsmen and soldiers who served and protected his territory; he was no longer the man who was struggling to feed his family; he went on to build a city for himself while his brother who stole both the birthright and the blessings was still wasting away serving for fourteen years for a wife and another extra six years of service in negotiation with his uncle before God's intervention for his deliverance and eventual escape with his wealth, wives and children.

When all odds seem against you, and the handwriting on the wall is clear even to a lame man who then tries to engage the gods in such a battle of wits for survival, not for the weak and the lily-livered but for the determined and the audacious men only. Though the Bible was silent on Esau and focused on Jacob, Esau did not allow that to deter him or distract him because he was not looking for people's authentication, approval or appraisal; he believed that his success and achievement would not only speak for him but will attract to him, attention and affection which has alluded him from his youth because of his past failures and mistakes, he now lived above hatred, forgot his past and focussed on his future, rediscover himself and the potential he has and this helped to bring out the best in him.

"And Jacob sent messengers before him to Esau his brother unto the land of Seir, the country of Edom. And he commanded them, saying, Thus shall ye speak unto my lord Esau; Thy servant Jacob saith thus, I have sojourned with Laban, and stayed there until now: And I have oxen, and asses, flocks, and men servants, and women servants: and I have sent to tell my lord, that I may find grace in thy sight." (Genesis 32:3-5)

Before you brag about your success and achievement, you must wait and see what others have done and achieved in the same period. Jacob was trying to impress his brother with what he had acquired in the past twenty years but was intimidated by the achievement of his brother Esau. Esau does not need the bribe or offer of appeasement sent to him by his brother, not because he was still bitter, but he saw no need because he had grown bigger and greater and was not impressed by Jacob's wealth.

"And the messengers returned to Jacob, saying, We came to thy brother Esau, and also he cometh to meet thee, and four hundred men with him. Then Jacob was greatly afraid and distressed: and he divided the people that was with him, and the flocks, and herds, and the camels, into two bands;" (Genesis 32:6-7)

Here comes a man who was once upon a time seen as a never-do-well, a nonentity and a failure escorted by four hundred men who were his foot soldiers, and nothing could be greater than this for a man who started with nothing, no inheritance, no connection, no parental blessings and no leverage upon which he started from just sheer determination born out of frustrations and rejections.

"Deliver me, I pray thee, from the hand of my brother, from the hand of Esau: for I fear him, lest he will come and smite me, and the mother with the children." (Genesis 32:11)

The fear of Esau here was the beginning of wisdom. Jacob sought help; he was led to prayers and sought divine intervention for deliverance from his brother's hand because of the injustice and betrayal the brother suffered from him. His conscience pricked him, and he had no rest within himself for fear of a reprisal attack; he was nervous and was trying to wear this bold face to cover his fear. So, he divided his wives, children and flocks into groups, fearing if one group was attacked, the other would survive; he was still seeing Esau with the old thoughts of an angry brother coming with an invading army on a revenge mission. It was this event that led Jacob to pray alone all night and have a wrestling bout with an angel while calling for help to avert the impending and imminent danger looming upon him and his family, he definitely needed help, and this help can only come from God, as he held onto the angel that if the angel doesn't bless him to change his situation, he will not let go.

"And say ye moreover, Behold, thy servant Jacob is behind us. For he said, I will appease him with the present that goeth before me, and afterward I will see his face; peradventure he will accept of me." (Genesis 32:20)

This was the result of guilt and self-condemnation for his past misdeeds to his brother. He was haunted by his past, and he is the one seeking forgiveness now by appeasement because the table has turned.

"And Jacob lifted up his eyes, and looked, and, behold, Esau came, and with him four hundred men. And he divided the children unto Leah, and unto Rachel, and unto the two handmaids. And he

put the handmaids and their children foremost, and Leah and her children after, and Rachel and Joseph hindermost. And he passed over before them, and bowed himself to the ground seven times, until he came near to his brother. And Esau ran to meet him, and embraced him, and fell on his neck, and kissed him: and they wept." (Genesis 33:1-4)

You can only appease an angry, bitter and resentful person, but Esau has gone past that level of unforgiveness which would have held him down and bound; he went out of his comfort zone, left his parents and wondered about until he broke the yolks of failure and poverty, the yolks of slavery and the yolk of servants. As Jacob approached, he bowed seven times before his brother Esau because of guilt and fear. Because he was intimidated by a man's success, wealth, and accomplishment, he duped off all blessings and inheritance. However, not wanting to embarrass him, Esau grabbed, embraced, kissed, and fell on his neck as they both wept. He surely has missed him and probably pitied his miserably small achievement despite all his manipulations.

"And he said, What meanest thou by all this drove which I met? And he said, These are to find grace in the sight of my lord. And Esau said, I have enough, my brother; keep that thou hast unto thyself. And Jacob said, Nay, I pray thee, if now I have found grace in thy sight, then receive my present at my hand: for therefore I have seen thy face, as though I had seen the face of God, and thou was pleased with me." (Genesis 33:8-10)

Now, the one deemed a failure has become the lord as the narrative changes; events, circumstances and situations can propel and motivate a failure to become an instant success. Out of fear and guilt, he persuaded his senior brother to take some gift from him as compensation for all the hurt and pain he has caused him; he now wants to find grace because Esau now has the power and the means to overrun and destroy Jacob and all that he has. It was indeed a show of force, with one being intimidated.

Coming to visit the one who betrayed you with four hundred soldiers? Nothing can be more frightening.

While Jacob sought to establish a tent for himself and his family in Bethel, Esau had already built a city where he was the chief of Edom in Seir. Why surrender to your adversaries to mock and run you down? Why are you always afraid of adversities? Learn from the man who was deemed not good enough, who has failed in so many things, a man who was doomed and bewitched by a malevolent spirit, a man who faced rejection and betrayal and yet overcame all to triumph and succeed where no one thought he could; there is no immunity against hardship and the challenges of life, but the more the battle you fight and won, the more the medal you are decorated with, the greater the glory, the greater the trouble, only those who endure the pain will enjoy the gain. Dare to be audacious.

CHAPTER 7
STARDOM

Stardom is the state of being very famous, having a celebrity status or prominence in a chosen field or profession.

The Star-dom is the actor stage, territory, domain, etc, where he has total and unrestricted domination where he rules and absolutely in his chosen career. They are professionals in their chosen area or field of work; they must be extremely good at what they do and at the top bracket, which makes them the envy of many, the symbol of success, role models to some, mentors and the desires of many young upcoming actors on the stage of life who covet greatness and honour who also wishes to be renown, distinct and excel as well.

Now, achieving and getting to the stage of stardom is a task and risk many dare not try, for the stake is big, the sacrifice is huge, the stage is massive, and the discipline required is second to none. This is the reason that only a few determined, stubborn, resilient and tenacious ones can survive while others silently and quietly withdraw, find excuses and surrender to faith, allowing the wind to take control of the boat of their destiny in the high sea of life and forced them to eventually dock at a wrong port, there they accept their newfound land and adjust to life there. Many set out in life with great dreams, aspirations, hopes and high expectations, but when the reality of life dawns on them, they accept their fate and cave in under immense pressure. Many wished and set out to be medical practitioners but ended up as laboratory attendants; many set up to be architects but ended up as bricklayers; many others aspired to be engineers but found themselves in the teaching profession, while many others ended their once-upon a time promising dream and vision to become bike riders, delivery drivers, uber drivers, these were never what they dreamt of, but they had to settle for this as a means of survival. What happened on the way from the beginning to where we all find ourselves today?

"Behold, I pray thee, the situation of this city is pleasant, as my lord seeth: but the water is naught, and the ground barren." (2 Kings 2:19)

Jericho was the biggest and the best entry point to the promised land, which was heralded with much fun fare and celebrations as the wall of the city fell miraculously, and they took possession of the land, which was said to be flowing with milk and honey. What happened to this once lovely, well-desired and fertile land during the course of time? The same affects humans in the process of time; we lose our bearing, our focus changes, we move the goalposts, we live in dreamlands, and finally, we give up to external forces who take over to manipulate and frustrate our destinies. Truly, our land needs healing, our water needs healing, and our destiny needs divine help to revive it and bring it back to life from where it is being confined.

Achieving stardom is giving your star domination to rule over a territory and become a force to be reckoned with, but if you fade out in the battle of survival, you become part of those who tried but could not thrive and might eventually live a peracetic life.

Not all stars shine, and not all stars mount up to the stage of stardom until they dominate territory or reign at the topmost level of their profession.

"Ye are the light of the world. A city that is set on an hill cannot be hid. Neither do men light a candle, and put it under a bushel, but on a candlestick, and it giveth light unto all that are in the house. Let your light so shine before men, that they may see your good works, and glorify your Father which is in heaven." (Matthew 5:14-16)

Light is not given to you just to illuminate yourself; you cannot fulfil destiny until you are able to shine out of darkness and until the whole world sees your light because the purpose of your existence is to be seen illuminating the world around you. You are required to make a difference as all focus would be on you as one who has God, and expectations are very high as they await your manifestations, and the will of God is for you to shine and illuminate others you have been given to give. As a city and a candle example given by Jesus, it is not all about getting lit but being well positioned to serve the people around you; light does not shine for itself but for others around it.

Once men are disconnected from their stars or separated by distance away from their stars, they will never fulfil their destinies until they are well stationed and well positioned where they have been destined to function. It might surprise you that most candles have been deliberately hidden in the bushel because of hatred, fear of exposure of their evil deeds and fear of you outshining them or overtaking them; there is also the fear of those who will benefit from your rising and shining but where victims of some strange powers and forces that never wanted them to get help and wanted them to be perpetually in darkness all the days of their lives, these are the reasons why many cannot survive the pressure, take the risk, meet the demands and the challenges confronting those who wish to achieve the status of stardom. Your duty is to shine and illuminate the world around you through your works being seen and your God being glorified through your acts of good service. Life is always for the rugged, the never give up, and those whose circumstances have taught a lesson and diverted their energy to achieve greatness instead of condemning themselves, being vengeful, bitter, or being abusers of drugs and alcohol. Dashed hope and failed expectations have frustrated many and led them to depression, and this consequently led them to addiction as a solution to a life-threatening tsunami that has swallowed up millions of those who became victims of their circumstances. These situations have killed many, maimed others and landed some in hospital beds confined for the rest of their lives due to mental and emotional stress.

"There is one glory of the sun, and another glory of the moon, and another glory of the stars: for one star differeth from another star in glory." (1 Corinthians 15:41)

This illustration proves that there is a hierarchy and there are orders in God's divine creation. As we cannot all be the same, there is beauty in diversity. Each one is a different design and a different brand created to serve a different purpose.

The glory of the sun is not the same as the glory of the moon, and each of them knows their time to shine, a time to shine in a particular territory without any hitch; they take turns to perform their duty and fulfil their assignment. Some of us are made to reign and shine in the morning, others will have their turn in the afternoon, and others flourish only at night in thick darkness when the circumstances and situations are conducive for their powers to flourish and dominate. There is an appointed time for each life bearer to shine and fulfil their existence's purpose; the stars' glory is not like that of the sun and the moon; stars are many, and they differ from each other in glory. This is proof we differ in our power and our ability to illuminate as you cannot compare halogen light with the electrical bulbs at home, neither can you compare the fluorescent with the streetlight so as they differ with one another in intensity so you cannot compare a star with other stars but no matter how dim a star shines, a star is still a star but not all stars can rise to the stage of stardom. Some will remain local champions, others will be street champions, some will be national champions, while some will illuminate the global stage.

"Arise, shine; for thy light is come, and the glory of the Lord is risen upon thee. For, behold, the darkness shall cover the earth, and gross darkness the people: but the Lord shall arise upon thee, and his glory shall be seen upon thee. And the Gentiles shall come to thy light, and kings to the brightness of thy rising." (Isaiah 60:1-3)

For the sun to rise, it must have set, and for a man to rise, he must have fallen; there is the going down of the sun, and there is the coming up of the sun at each appointed time. Those who don't devise a means of rising after a fall can never rise and shine. Arise is a charge, a call, a challenge to everyone to come out of obscurity to the limelight from failures, addictions, poverty, indebtedness and from where life's wrestlers have knocked you down by a technical knockout.

Knowing fully well that success is the product of failure, and prosperity is a product of poverty, and light was also called out of darkness, all victories are the product of battles and challenges. Once your appointed times come and you don't take your chance, you might never make it again unless you are one of those specially gifted, anointed, or fortunate enough to get multiple opportunities because opportunity once lost might not be recovered. At your appointed time, the glory of God will meet your rising light, and the combination of the two will lift you to stardom.

Darkness is a necessity for the rise of each star, for their recognition and manifestations. Light is of no importance where there is no darkness; it is the darkness that brings out the beauty and the relevance of light, and for the glory of God to be seen upon you, you, too, must have reason to intensify your light. Where was the glory before you rose? It is your rising that provides the platform upon which the glory of God will rest; God will not send out his glory into a vacuum.

"And the light shineth in darkness; and the darkness comprehended it not." (John 1:5)

Until you know the importance of darkness and rise above the power of darkness as Christ Jesus did when his light shone while being surrounded by darkness; Jesus waited for thirty years, he set the bar high, he met God's expectations, and he prevailed when tempted to compromise before his illumination and manifestations. When the glory of God falls upon a rising man whose light has already been illuminated and the appointed time has come for such a person to shine if rightly positioned in a good location and a good environment that is not hostile to his manifestations, he shines.

The Gentiles coming to your light shows you that God's glory, success, stardom, greatness, wealth etc are not a product of any religious jingoism, ethnic or cultural barriers but divine arrangement for God's perfect work for humanity to be fulfilled through his chosen vessels of honour, this shows that achieving stardom invites, attracts, commands respect and draws the attention of even the high and the mighty, the king and their queens and the movers and shakers of society to your feet.

"Thou shalt also suck the milk of the Gentiles, and shalt suck the breast of kings: and thou shalt know that I the Lord am thy Saviour and thy Redeemer, the mighty One of Jacob." (Isaiah 60:16)

Since success has a set standard and class, exclusive to executives and those who have weathered the storm to arrive at the upper chambers echelon of their chosen career or profession, people, kings and queens have no choice but to come with their substance to celebrate success, victory and stardom.

"And this is the condemnation, that light is come into the world, and men loved darkness rather than light, because their deeds were evil. For every one

that doeth evil hateth the light, neither cometh to the light, lest his deeds should be reproved." (John 3:19-20)

This shows that the moment you are in the inescapable light, we will shine and expose the deeds of the nocturnal beings who revelled and thrived under the shadow of thick darkness for fear of being seen, condemned, criticised and attacked; they then engage in their assignment of causing havoc and all destructive gimmicks to stop the star from shining and put an end to their nefarious activities.

This is not a fight for supremacy because light needs only to be switched on and set up in the right position and at the right time to shine. There is no contest, no compromise, no negotiation until you shine.

Getting to the top is much easier than remaining at the top. Maintaining a top position requires more than gifts, degrees, and skills, just as marrying a woman is much easier than keeping a woman in a relationship. The requirements are too enormous, and only the determined can afford to pay them.

"And it waxed great, even to the host of heaven; and it cast down some of the host and of the stars to the ground, and stamped upon them." (Daniel 8:10)

The moment you rise, you will no longer operate in obscurity once your star is seen, once you are known and heard by many who didn't know of your existence before, all suddenly will now start to judge you, to condemn you and to intimidate you until you give up your stardom status.

"And they that be wise shall shine as the brightness of the firmament; and they that turn many to righteousness as the stars forever and ever." (Daniel 12:3)

The wise, the discerned and the men of Issachar's vision are those who endure the tests of time and come out as survivors. Have you heard the slogan 'time will tell'? Tell what? If you want to be on the global stage for a long time and continue to enjoy stardom, if you will fade out eventually, or if you will remain relevant as time goes on. If you don't become one of the victims of a satanic set-up to bring you down, can you endure the weapons thrown at you that you will survive against all odds that will rise to confront you?

The best in you cannot be brought out, and the worst in you cannot be stirred up until an external force provokes you; it is like the law of inertia, which states that every object at rest will remain at rest and an object in motion will continue in motion with a constant velocity unless acted upon by an external force. If you are not facing any obstacles, no obstructions, no rejection, no frustrations or being sacked at your place of work, you will not come out of your comfort zone to confront the challenges ahead; hence, the best in you cannot be revealed until you lose that which you thought is the best, you cannot know the best is yet to come, still in your mind waiting to be unlocked. So, when under serious provocation, your spirit is stirred up, holy anger or bitterness will move you to one form of addiction or the other, addiction to the good or the bad, prayer addiction, reading addiction, alcohol addiction, drug addictions and all form of addictions both good and bad seeking a way to fill the vacuums left behind by their loss.

However, this anger moves many to vent their anger improving their lots and to be better in life, they then develop anger driven success which leads to excellence and intellectual prowess in their chosen field while the same anger will cause some to vent their anger on everyone around them playing the victims instead of using the opportunity to make their life better and not bitter.

Therefore, it's a matter of choice on where you channel your energy during those periods. Those who made it to the top did not get to the top because they merely wished or desired to be at the top, but they aspired to acquire that which they wanted, overcoming all challenges and coming out of the tunnel of darkness to the light we've been taught is at the 'end of the tunnel'.

Furthermore, stardom is more than a dream because many dreamers fade before their dreams are actualised. Erroneously, people believed that the gift of dreams and interpretations took Joseph to the top hierarchy in the land of Egypt; no, many have had their dreams stolen but have not learnt to go back to bed to sleep again and to have a new dream, gifts alone cannot get you to stardom until you have some other supportive rare qualities and attributes. The main thing that took Joseph to that position was the solution he proffers to the dreams of Pharoah. After the interpretation of the dream, he went further to analyse how they should go about executing the solution which he laid down, to which the king quickly alluded that they could not find any other man that could fill that specification, quality, and such divine wisdom among his people than Joseph himself, so the obvious choice was Joseph.

In life, you are either the problem to be solved, part of the problem to be solved, or the creator of the problem, or you are the solution to problems created by others. If you are the solution to peoples' problems, no matter where you are, you'll be sought out because the world needs men like you who have solutions to the barrage of problems confronting humanity. The more the problem you solve, the greater you become in life and the more relevant as well; the challenges and obstacles you face and overcome and the battles you fight and win determine how well men will treat you and how much you will be decorated when you attain stardom.

"For a great door and effectual is opened unto me, and there are many adversaries." (1 Corinthians 16:9)

This is a factual statement that applies to everyone and proves that you don't attain greatness and stardom by chance, luck and unplanned; there are battles to be fought and won, and there are adversaries and adversities one after the other coming after you whenever the doors you knocked are opened, it opens another can of worms for another phase of troublers to come after you. For every opportunity or open door, many are the opposers and resistors who won't want you to enjoy your newfound success; that is, you mustn't rest on your oars because the success of yesterday won't be relevant tomorrow unless you continue to make more successful moves. There is no room for complacency and passiveness; continue to strive for the best every day as long as it is called today.

Breakthrough in life is the art of burrowing or breaking through obstacles and barriers to cross to the other side of the divide, like breaking through poverty to prosperity, failure to success, darkness to light, etc. All this requires much effort and resilience to achieve set goals. There is no retreat, no surrender.

CHAPTER 8
WEAPON OF MASS DESTRUCTION

The tongue is a weapon which, over the years, has been used to defame, destroy, break down, destabilise, abuse, slander, body shame and traumatise many great men in the battle of life, leading them to mental patience. The tongue has maimed and killed more people than the swords and arrows of warriors in battle. Are you a victim of the wounds and injuries caused by bitter words from bitter people? These arrows are shot daily, even in the absence of war; it has led many to their untimely deaths aided by social media platforms and other means of communication; the shooters of bitter words derive joy, happiness, and fulfilment from the impact of their utterances on their victims, they plan it, find people of like-minds to join them, they go all out of their ways to execute their plans, they get more excitement and joy from such a task just to belittle others, bring them down to the same level as themselves and frustrate their purpose. These are people who have failed in life, in marriage, in business, and in other fields of endeavours and are now carrying venoms of vipers. Not wanting to celebrate winners, they go all out to make a campaign of calumny just to level everyone and bring everyone to their level of bitterness.

Successful people don't give attention to every dog that barks at them on their way to glory; they see them as distractions, while some others see them as side-attractions and they give attention to them, thereby losing focus of their dreams or slowing them down completely which results in a journey of one year taking ten because they give attention to every unnecessary event all around them forgetting that those who want to be watched never become a watcher or spectator when they're supposed to be the main actor. Many have bled, cried, wept, and nursed wounds from every arsenal and weapon thrown at them but never see reasons to give up the fight; that is, the spirit of the warriors. When one is shot in the battle of life, removing the bullet stuck in our flesh shouldn't be our priority, but to continue the fight even with the pain in our flesh until the end of the battle. We must keep fighting the opposition despite our wounds and injuries. We often get pricked on the wounds or scars, and the bleeding starts again. It's only those few who can survive such a fierce battle of endurance can live to tell the story of their experiences; today, many still go about with bullets in their body tissues and yet have refused to give up. Many will read history, but few will make history; the making of history is not only about suffering because many are suffering today and will suffer for the rest of their lives and will never make history because no one is interested in the story of a failure.

Our tears from deep bitterness and deep tissue wounds have often taken too long to heal because we have refused to agree to the terms and conditions laid down for peace by our adversaries.

"Why is my pain perpetual, and my wound incurable, which refuseth to be healed?" (Jeremiah 15:18)

"Woe is me for my hurt! my wound is grievous; but I said, Truly this is a grief, and I must bear it." (Jeremiah 10:19)

Many, who go about with injuries, bleeding, bullets in their body, and brokenness in their hearts without any hope of healing from anywhere and yet become warriors for not giving up on their divine assignment.

"Hide me from the secret counsel of the wicked; from the insurrection of the workers of iniquity: Who whet their tongue like a sword, and bend their bows to shoot their arrows, even bitter words: That they may shoot in secret at the perfect: suddenly do they shoot at him, and fear not. They encourage themselves in an evil matter: they commune of

laying snares privily; they say, Who shall see them?" (Psalm 64:2-5)

The wicked don't have to buy arms and ammunition to destroy their victims; they have a weapon already in them; they only whet their tongues, devise evil upon beds, conspire and take counsel targeting their victims who are unaware of their evil plans as they innocently fall victims of these backbiters who will do anything to get accomplice with whom they form a rebellion and a force of resistance to the advancement and progress of others.

Do you wonder how they get their victims? Yeah, those who are better, more accepted with better accomplishments, more loved, making waves, more successful, enjoying special favour, specially gifted, or those with common grace are prime targets for bitter words and are good victims for bullies who believe they don't deserve to be where they are, who they are and what they have, they employ themselves trying to convince others to hate those whom they hate and to join them in their mission of mass destruction.

"My soul is among lions: and I lie even among them that are set on fire, even the sons of men, whose teeth are spears and arrows, and their tongue a sharp sword." (Psalm 57:4)

They are then set on fire, ready to devour and consume their victims into total extinction; their teeth are said to be spears, and their tongues are sharp swords with which they hunt down their unsuspecting prey. Their greatest and most important device is lies; they lie against many in judgment just to get them eliminated from the scene as they are seen as hindrances to their existence or well-being and must be destroyed at all costs.

"For the mouth of the wicked and the mouth of the deceitful are opened against me: they have spoken against me with a lying tongue. They compassed me about also with words of hatred; and fought against me without a cause." (Psalm 109:2-3)

These lies were born and fabricated out of hatred and not because of any fault, sin or misdeed because you can never behave well before those who hate you, there will always be an explanation, misinterpretation and misunderstanding of everything you say just to get people to support them to fulfil their mission.

"Deliver my soul, O Lord, from lying lips, and from a deceitful tongue. What shall be given unto thee? or what shall be done unto thee, thou false tongue? Sharp arrows of the mighty, with coals of juniper." (Psalm 120:2-4)

Deceitful tongues and false tongues are like snakes that cannot be appeased once they rear their ugly head or when they're interested in you. The sharp arrows with coals of junipers show the potency of their warhead and their destructive intents; no appeasement can change the mind of a hater, even buying them a car or building them a house will appease them unless you give them your back to ride on and give up your dreams for theirs even if it is too big for them to shoulder.

My people believe you can have a sacrifice of appeasement for the gods, the spirits, the witches or wizards when offended or provoked, but no one has found a suitable and well-accepted way or sacrifice to calm down a raging fiery tongue which is set to burn down a whole generational success.

"Deliver me, O Lord, from the evil man: preserve me from the violent man; Which imagine mischiefs in their heart; continually are they gathered together for war. They have sharpened their tongues like a serpent; adders' poison is under their lips. Selah. Keep me, O Lord, from the hands of the wicked; preserve me from the violent man; who have purposed to overthrow my goings." (Psalm 140:1-4)

They are violent, desperate, fierce, unrepentant, forceful, and horrific, as they threaten, frighten and intimidate people using every available form of communication to achieve their set objectives of character assassination and set many against their supposed enemies. They imagine mischief and conspiracy in their mind and come up with an idea of execution aided by men of like minds and promoted by fools and accepted by ignorance who were only having fun or cruising on other people's matters. That which is making someone cry uncontrollably is what is counted as fun to others.

"Their throat is an open sepulchre; with their tongues they have used deceit; the poison of asps is under their lips: Whose mouth is full of cursing and bitterness: Their feet are swift to shed blood: Destruction and misery are in their ways:" (Romans 3:13-16)

The tongue is not only set as a fiery sword but also whetted with the poison of asps, used for deceit, lying, bearing false witness, cursing and pouring out bitterness, which is stored in the heart, as the bible says, from the abundance of the heart the mouth speaks. Haters will do anything to bring others down; they don't think of the negative impacts of their words on their victims and the consequences of death, rejection, mental torture, trauma, loneliness, hatred and the frustrations which their victims will be subjected to long after they have executed their plans, they don't care as long as they achieve their destructive aims.

The star must endure many known and unknown arrows flying from every direction to puncture, abort, terminate or frustrate their illumination or total elimination from existence. Only the strong, the rugged and the never-say-die will survive despite all odds against them, while many others will give up after a shot or arrow hits them on the battlefield.

The tongues almost destroyed the vision of God for Joseph as his master's wife lied against him, which eventually landed him in jail for an offence he had not committed. The tongue was the only weapon used in the destruction of Naboth when he insisted on not giving up or selling his inheritance to King Ahab, but Ahab, through his wife Jezebel's well-executed lies, eventually led to his death, and Ahab inherited his family land.

Also, several times in the Psalmist's account, we can deduce that David, too, was traumatised and victimised by bitter words from deceitful tongues raised against his person to bring him to distribute before those who love him.

In the book of Proverbs, King Solomon likens it to 'the piercing of a sword'. Hatred, afflictions, and ruins are their trademarks; they never give up until their target is destroyed.

"...Come, and let us smite him with the tongue..." (Jeremiah 18:18)

Some words are words in seasons; they come at the appropriate time, and people blindly fall for them because they are sweet, melodious, comforting, soothing, and meet their immediate needs. However, those words could hide behind some hidden agenda of destruction or be meant to catch their victims before subjecting them to the pain, agony, and trauma they make their victims go through.

"The words of his mouth were smoother than butter, but war was in his heart: his words were softer than oil, yet were they drawn swords." (Psalm 55:21)

These are like wolves in sheep's clothing, which some of us blindly and gladly accept as we open up to them in our brokenness, only to be left more broken and devastated than ever before; in our brokenness, we are preoccupied with finding a comforter than to discern the voice of the deceitful, only the survivors live to tell the story of such bitter experiences of those who took advantage of other people's vulnerability to inflict further injuries on them after promising them heaven on earth. Have you ever been jilted by a loved one? From the onset, they knew what they wanted, and after using you and abusing you, they left you to yourself to bear the pain alone and lick your wounds. This is not peculiar to any particular gender; it is all about personal experiences, which generally differ from one person to another.

"Behold, they belch out with their mouth: swords are in their lips..." (Psalm 59:7)

The conspiracy plan is to remove others from their excellency and reduce them to nothing. The mouth, the lips, and the tongues are the fiercest partnerships in the human body, and they can set a whole family against themselves and a whole nation on fire. They have been responsible for every war and battle fought from time immemorial.

"Even so the tongue is a little member, and boasteth great things. Behold, how great a matter a little fire kindleth! And the tongue is a fire, a world of iniquity: so is the tongue among our members, that it defileth the whole body, and setteth on fire the course of nature; and it is set on fire of hell." (James 3:5-6)

The tongue is one of the greatest weapons all men possess, but the man who uses it irrationally lives to reap and regret his utterances. He who opens his mouth too often will soon find himself in soup. The tongue is a spark that can set the whole house on fire, set people against themselves, turn siblings and relatives against one another, make enemies out of friends, make people bitter and vengeful as well as make some seem unworthy through cyberbullying, body shaming, abusive words, demining words, derogatory words, verbal abuse, social media fracas etc and some of the destructive attributes of the tongue, which has left many devastated. James says further, 'but the tongue can no man tame. It's an unruly evil, full of deadly poison'. The tongue is the only potent weapon that has led many to battle and kills many without the use of a bullet.

"A good man out of the good treasure of the heart bringeth forth good things: and an evil man out of the evil treasure bringeth forth evil things. But I say unto you, That every idle word that men shall speak, they shall give account thereof in the day of judgment. For by thy words thou shalt be justified, and by thy words thou shalt be condemned." (Matthew 12:35-37)

Ask yourself, as one who possesses this weapon of mass destruction, are you a victim of the tongue, or are you the one victimising others?

CHAPTER 9
DOWN BUT NOT OUT

Sometimes, the circumstances and challenges we encounter on the way become so enormous that we get knocked down several times but refusing to give up is the slogan to employ in such a dear situation, several times in the process of making progress, many fall and sustain various degrees of burns, injuries and wounds but since time heals all wounds, they only needed enough time to refresh, to recoup, to regroup, to get reinforcements and launch out again. We all need time for healing and recovery after a fall in the battle of life; then, we need to re-strategise, re-energise and reorder our priorities before we dabble into the waters for another round of the challenge. We should always learn from our mistakes, pick the lessons from our mistakes, and make better decisions in our subsequent attempts to get better results.

"Our soul is escaped as a bird out of the snare of the fowlers: the snare is broken, and we are escaped." (Psalm 124:7)

When the enemies eventually catch their victims to feed on them, only the divine intervention of God can break the evil nets of the adversaries and put an end to their celebrations and joy over their victims.

Once upon a time, even the most decorated warrior of all time – King David – was caught with his pants down, and there was no escape. He was made to face the music, public ridicule, and shame as he was shamefully chased away from the throne and fled before his son. Though David was down but was not totally forsaken by God, he arose again from the ashes, came out of the rubble of his fall and rose again to greatness. He learnt his lesson and never repeated the same mistake, which brought reproach and embarrassment to him by the adversaries in the presence of his subjects who thought he was a perfect, faultless and impeccable angel.

Are you in your lowest moment and down? God has always lifted the downtrodden who looked up to him in times of trouble; he turned their ashes to beauty, and if he had done it before, he could have done it again. If only we could put him in again.

"Knowing that he which raised up the Lord Jesus shall raise up us also by Jesus, and shall present us with you." (2 Corinthians 4:14)

"For which cause we faint not; but though our outward man perish, yet the inward man is renewed day by day. For our light affliction, which is but for a moment, worketh for us a far more exceeding and eternal weight of glory;" (2 Corinthians 4:16-17)

Afflictions are light and momentary, just a passing phase of a fraction of our lives; we are assured of a way of escape as we continue to encourage one another in the race for the trophy and the crown of winners. A far and exceedingly great crown of glory that outweighs our suffering awaits every winner who endures pain to the end.

God is not an unjust God who creates without plans and purpose; every one of his creations has been designed to perform a particular task and to excel in the process. No one was designed to fail, but man fails when we fail to continue because of failure. When a horse knocks down the rider, he dusts himself and learns how to mount the horse again, passing across to the horse a message that you are the Lord over it and are in charge. Through what we go through, we are expected to learn and cultivate some peculiar habits and traits which cannot be learnt but earned from experience through endurance, tolerance, perseverance, self-control, patience, persistence, consistency, determination and being indefatigable.

"...after he had patiently endured, he obtained the promise." (Hebrews 6:15)

Apostle James encourages his readers to endure, saying endurance will earn you approval and eventually the crown of life, as only those tested are approved and trusted. Your patience must have perfect words to obtain the coveted crown of glory. You may also wonder why the word of God admonishes us to 'count it all joy' when we are thrown in the fire, among the thorns, in the lion's den, in hard and harsh conditions, in the waters and in a very dangerous wilderness filled with wild animals. Why do we have to count persecutions and afflictions as joy if not for the result, which brings glory to God and blessings to man? It is because we have been charged not to see these things as something happening to us alone; when we look around, we will notice that everyone is immersed in one problem or the other as it is common knowledge that everyone, irrespective of their faith, race, gender or culture must pass through this phase at one point of their lives or the other. The next question is: why only me? Why do the nations rage? Why are the demons on a rampage, and the spirits are agitated to destroy someone who seems to be innocent?

"Beloved, think it not strange concerning the fiery trial which is to try you, as though some strange thing happened unto you:" (1 Peter 4:12)

This is proof that you are not alone; others are just going through theirs in silence without a fuss or making any drama of their own experiences, no pity party because the people you expect pity from might even be going through something worse than you or have just survived something. Someone says, 'You don't know what I'm going through,' and The other person says, 'You don't know where I'm coming from'. We all have to pass through to get through to our destinations; it is never something strange or peculiar to you; hard times, tough times, and seasons of difficulties breed great leaders because the difficulties they pass through have defined and tested their ruggedness and fighting spirit. These are the experiences of everyone in life who wants to be a trailblazer, achieve set goals, and succeed. Tough times, they say, don't last, but tough people do endure and survive tough times.

"...to establish you, and to comfort you concerning your faith: That no man should be moved by these

afflictions: for yourselves know that we are appointed thereunto." (1 Thessalonians 3:2-3)

No shaking, no qualms and no fear because we've been forewarned to be forearmed of the challenges ahead of us, and God has prepared us for the test of life because he doesn't want us to be failures.

"They are brought down and fallen: but we are risen, and stand upright." (Psalm 20:8)

For the sun to rise, it must first go down or set; for a man to rise, he must have fallen. But when God lifts them or brings them up after every fall, their adversaries are made to fall as they are displaced and replaced. God has not finished with you; you will definitely rise again.

CHAPTER 10
HALL OF FAME

To qualify to be listed in the hall of fame by all ramifications, you must have passed through the furnace of affliction, shed countless tears of sorrow and agony, and also bled on several occasions from the wounds sustained from the battles, challenges, and encounters one has gone through. One must have come, seen, participated, fought and won even when no one gave them the opportunity and no one believed in them. What terminated the dreams of others consumed many others and frightened some to total submission to the status quo they have lived above.

Dare to be different? Then you are on course to be listed in the galleries of the famous and the greatest of all times, which today are called 'G.O.A.T.s' in your chosen career, in your family or your generation, you must have made a difference and added value to people's lives. These great individuals have changed the course of history of their people, their generation and family through their acts of boldness, confidence and bravery to challenge authorities, fight against principalities, fight for freedom by risking their lives, give up their comforts, sacrifice everything, paid the ultimate price and were rewarded for their bravery.

"Who through faith subdued kingdoms, wrought righteousness, obtained promises, stopped the mouths of lions. Quenched the violence of fire, escaped the edge of the sword, out of weakness were made strong, waxed valiant in fight, turned to flight the armies of the aliens. Women received their dead raised to life again: and others were tortured, not accepting deliverance; that they might obtain a better resurrection: And others had trial of cruel mockings and scourgings, yea, moreover of bonds and imprisonment: They were stoned, they were sawn asunder, were tempted, were slain with the sword: they wandered about in sheepskins and goatskins; being destitute, afflicted, tormented;" (Hebrews 11:33-37)

Who else can subdue the kingdom and stop the rampaging mouth of a lion? Who has just been denied a sumptuous meal of lamb like the man King David? Who else could quench the fiery fire of the furnace seven times hotter than usual? Only brave men of Shadrach, Meshach and Abednego could dare to break the King's order in the midst of multitudes who compromised and complied without raising an eyebrow. These three men, who defiled the King's order, were subsequently saved miraculously, and the King himself admitted that no other god can deliver his people like the God of Shadrach, Meshach, and Abednego, and a decree was made to that effect.

Escaping the edge of the sword and the gallows erected as Mordecai and David escaped from the sword of King Saul and that of the Philistine giant called Goliath, these people were made strong out of weaknesses by the things they went through, 'for my strength is made perfect in weakness says the Lord'.

Jacob waxed valiantly, even against the angel of the Lord, to change the course of his history when he was displeased with the trend of events in his life, as the true manifestation of his name affected his personality.

Abram left the known for the unknown as he separated himself from his people, land, and inheritance. He dedicated himself to following God in a futuristic land. Also, despite the deadness of their bodies and the circumstances of the couple yet, they held onto God's promises and confessed their faith as they were being addressed as father and mother of nations even in their state of barrenness.

Remember also how Moses refused to be seen and addressed as a prince of Pharoah, a position many would have gladly preferred, but he chose to identify with the afflicted people of Israel in Egypt, having the awareness he was a born leader who would one day positively affect the course of their history.

Rehab was a well-known harlot in the city of Jericho but risked her life to hide and protect the Israelite spies, thus saving herself, her family and posterity to judge her sacrifices, and she got listed in the hall of faith despite being a harlot.

Their people are many others that time will not permit me to mention who took risks, made sacrifices, endured the process, and eventually reached their expected ends. Where there is no goal, there is no vision; without vision, no mission will be accomplished. Twenty-two men cannot be running after a round object called a football without a goalpost; if they do, there will be no winner, and there will be no goal; no matter how well they play and how long they play for, only a set goal is achievable.

In life, don't let those who have not fought a particular battle teach you how to fight yours. He who has never lived with a wife should not teach you how to enjoy your marital life; life is theoretical and practical, and the word of God should be practically applied to all situations. You cannot win a battle you have never fought, nor can you overcome what you have not gone through. To overcome poverty, you must have tasted and gone through poverty and survived. For you to tell your experience of betrayal, you must have been a victim of betrayal, so he who is removing the armour of war is not the same as he who is just wearing it and not sure if he will survive and return back home to share the experiences of the battle. No wonder King Solomon says in scripture, 'the end of a matter is better than the beginning' because many start the race for glory, but only a few survive to be glorified, just like in a marathon, many run, but few get to the finishing line, and very few wins the competition.

Your anointing, election, appointment, or random selection is just the beginning of the process, and only the tough will eventually make it to the top. Only one governor governs a state, only one president or prime minister rules a nation, and only one King reigns within a kingdom; this is to prove to you that space at the top is not only limited and restricted but only for the reserved very, very important personalities. What makes them prominent and stand out and makes them essential is not their age because they ruled over people much older than them, not their education either because they governed people who are not only more intellectual, more educated than them, not even because of their gifts, talents or skills because they have many subjects in their kingdom like Daniel in the palace when it comes to the matter of spirituality. Also, they are not even the richest, yet they make rules and decrees that affect those worthier than them and yet are obeyed ahead in high esteem because of what they have been through to get them to where they are which the older, the richer and the more gifted dare not attempt for fear of death.

Now, to the secular world and some of our local examples, we see people like Oprah Winfrey, J.K. Rowling and Howard Schultz, who said 'when I was seven years old, I experienced something that deeply affected me that I carry with me every single day and that is the scar and the shame of being a poor kid living in government subsidised housing'. Martin Luther King jr, Barrack Obama, and so many others fought against racial discrimination, bullies, mental abuse and rejection and still excelled to get to the pinnacle of their chosen careers.

The adversaries attack you for who you are and what threat you pose to their own established dynasty and kingdom. That is why they put on the pressure of continuous attacks until the lily-livered succumbs to their intimidations.

Your future is more important than your past, they can only use your past to haunt you in order to destroy what is left of your future, but as Joseph said, "as for you, ye thought evil against me, but God meant it unto good". So, take solace in that word of Joseph that what was designed to destroy you, God will surely turn around for your good if you don't give up on your dreams and if you don't become victims of their devices.

In closing this chapter, there are scars that definitely qualify so many people to the Hall of Fame, at least for their family, nation or tribe, if not globally. When I see the scars below the abdomen of my wife, it reminds me of the pain and sorrow she thrice went through, through childbirth as she went through caesarean section operations just to give life to three beautiful children, and so is the case of so many other women who were cut open and who had various tears just to bear children. As men, we don't take this for granted because these sacrifices were made to fulfil the purpose and be counted among mothers, and this gave the men the opportunity to be called fathers, which would not be possible without someone going through the pain. The scars speak to me, and I understand the pain and the history behind those scars.

CHAPTER 11
PANECEA

> *"And Jesus answering said, A certain man went down from Jerusalem to Jericho, and fell among thieves, which stripped him of his raiment, and wounded him, and departed, leaving him half dead. And by chance there came down a certain priest that way: and when he saw him, he passed by on the other side. And likewise a Levite, when he was at the place, came and looked on him, and passed by on the other side. But a certain Samaritan, as he journeyed, came where he was: and when he saw him, he had compassion on him, And went to him, and bound up his wounds, pouring in oil and wine, and set him on his own beast, and brought him to an inn, and took care of him. And on the morrow when he departed, he took out two pence, and gave them to the host, and said unto him, Take care of him; and whatsoever thou spendest more, when I come again, I will repay thee." (Luke 10:30-35)*

The above parables speak of the despicable travail of most of us in our day-to-day activities and encounters. We often come across dangerous, evil-minded, wicked beasts in human skin and in some precarious, unavoidable situations. Many are fallen victims among thieves, night marauders, armed robbers of destinies, and glory hunters, and we find no way out but to endure the persecutions and afflictions meted out to us.

Just like this man above, in our quest for a better life, we come across situations and people who stripped us of honour, glory, wealth, and dignity and robbed us of our valuables, leaving us not only naked but got us beaten to the state of stupor. This man was wounded all over his body and left for dead; his perceived lifeless body was abandoned by the wayside, gasping for breath if there could be any hope of revival and survival.

Unfortunately, those who we expect and look up to for help in such a season as this passes by never want to be seen or identified with our broken-blooded bodies. They cross over to the other side of the road to avoid being linked with the crime or being charged for what he knows nothing about, though he was a priest, a pious and religious man whose reputation must not be stained but sustained. He, therefore, chooses to look away and take another route to his destination, leaving the victim in the pool of blood.

Then came another would-be helper on the same route but of lesser religious authority than the first man; he went as far as coming close to the victim and having a close look to determine how severe the injury was and to be sure if the man was still breathing or dead. After confirming the information, he needed to tell other people in the city what befell a man he found on the way, he too crossed over to the other side and went his way.

Many times, friends, families and neighbours would enquire about your well-being, job, and schooling just for the sake of asking because, after your explanations and narrations, all you hear is 'God will send you help', but they will never do anything to help you. You wonder why they ask questions, and you keep explaining yourself, looking for help where there is none, as they all leave you the way they met you.

However, the person who was least expected to assist the victim of this robbery attack was passing through the same route that others passed through, saw what they saw and spotted the need to help the helpless man in a pool of his blood; he came closer, he looked deeper and saw the man was between life and death and chose to have compassion on him, that was what the others who saw him before him lacked even though they saw his predicaments and the need to help him. The helper of the victims was the Samaritans, who were labelled an impure and corrupted race, and no Jew wanted to associate with them. Yet, he breaks the racial barrier and religious and cultural divisions separating the Jews and the Samaritans by offering to assist a Jew in trouble regardless of the animosity and the hatred the Jews have for them.

This Samaritan is a good example of Christ Jesus – who came and had compassion on most of us who are fallen victims of circumstances on our way in the wilderness of life, struggling for survival and recovery among thieves and robbers. Help came at last as the man bound up his wound after the application of ethanol as a disinfectant and cleanser of the wound sustained in that life-threatening encounter; he later poured oil on the wound to soothe and hasten healing.

He went on further to rescue him from the scene of the incident after administering first aid and subsequently set him on his beast and took him to an inn to be taken care of by the owner and the operators of the inn – which today could be a private hospital to be given the best of treatment, to stop the bleeding and save the life of a victim with a circumstance. He lodged at the same inn that night, ensuring all things were well in place for the care of a total stranger. On the second day, before his departure, he paid not only for the cost of treatment incurred overnight but for subsequent treatment to be administered to the man.

"Take care of him" is how Christ Jesus has seen us in dire situations, rescued us, and brought us to a safe place to be fed, treated, and looked after by good shepherds. He pays for the past, present and future services to be rendered; though the damage has been done, he is a repairer who mends and heals all brokenness and takes them to a safe place to fulfil purpose. He has taken it upon himself for whatever he spent healing our brokenness and mental and emotional sicknesses. He cares and would not fail nor forsake those who trust him, as he is still helping the destitute.

"How God anointed Jesus of Nazareth with the Holy Ghost and with power: who went about doing good, and healing all that were oppressed of the devil; for God was with him." (Acts 10:38)

Help is coming at last to those whom the world condemns because of their sins; he is out to forgive and bring up the downtrodden, for that is the purpose of his anointing to set free the oppressed from their oppressors.

"He healeth the broken in heart, and bindeth up their wounds." (Psalm 147:3)

This is an assurance that our help is around the corner because God is always ready and willing to help those who are not afraid, who are not ashamed of asking for help in their state of helplessness and those who admit they need help to get out of a situation.

"...When the enemy shall come in like a flood, the Spirit of the Lord shall lift up a standard against him." (Isaiah 59:19)

Most times, the help doesn't come when you want it and as you expected it to end all the problems, but the most timely help is to help you survive in the midst of the problem without being consumed. God did not bring Shadrach, Meshach, and Abednego out of the fire but kept them alive and untouched neither did he bring Daniel out of the den but kept him alive amid the lion, leaving those who put them in the problem to bring them out themselves, God works miracles in diverse ways.

"When thou passest through the waters, I will be with thee; and through the rivers, they shall not overflow thee: when thou walkest through the fire, thou shalt not be burned; neither shall the flame kindle upon thee." (Isaiah 43:2)

This shows God's methodology of helping us to survive what was meant to put an end to our existence. All this proves he never comes to bring us out of every trouble. Still, we have the assurance that he will stand by us, teach us, protect us, train us to be strong and prepare us for leadership challenges. Ultimately, God wants to be glorified in every situation. He does this in diverse ways; in God's deliverance and salvation plans, his glorification is paramount. He won't do anything that won't bring glory, testimonies and thanksgiving to his name. Even if the affliction or trouble resulted from our disobedience, he still cares when we call on him in humility as Jonah did in the belly of the fish.

Despite the death sentences being passed unto all the Jews as someone who hated them had paid for their lives during the time of Esther, the fervent and effective prayers of the saints avails much, and God heard them, and their deliverance was unprecedented.

Furthermore, the affliction of every child of God was depicted through the analogy of "the bush was burning with fire, but the bush was not consumed". Nothing says it better as we lament and cry out for help in the midst of the burning fire, but here we are, not consumed and not looking like what we have been through because his grace was made perfect in our weaknesses. The fire of the enemies has refined us, purified us, making us glitter, shine, dazzle and become better and greater than we would ever have been.

Every enemy is a promoter and a catalyst that has been used to push us out of our perceived comfort zone to a higher and better place God has designed for us. Without a push, no one takes a leap into the unknown when God lifts you up; no one brings you down, but when you cut corners by jumping up, the force of gravity will bring you down again. A word is enough for the wise.

"Persecutions, afflictions, which came unto me at Antioch, at Iconium, at Lystra; what persecutions I endured: but out of them all the Lord delivered me. Yea, and all that will live godly in Christ Jesus shall suffer persecution." (2 Timothy 3:11-12)

Be prepared, no matter the situations and circumstances that you've been subjected to by those who hate you and desire to eliminate you at all costs, God is still on the throne and still in the business of deliverance for those who call upon him in distress, pick up your phone and dial his number in prayers, he still answers distress calls. He knows when to come for you before things get out of hand; he has always made a way of escape for everyone being tried, tested or tempted and never allows them to be drawn and pulled beyond their elastic limit.

"For ye need patience, that, after ye have done the will of God, ye might receive the promise. For yet a

little while, and he that shall come will come, and will not tarry." (Hebrews 10:36-37)

Finally, brethren, I urge you to wait patiently for him, who has promised you because he remains faithful to his words, remembers his promises, and will definitely come at his appointed time on his terms and conditions.

GALLERY

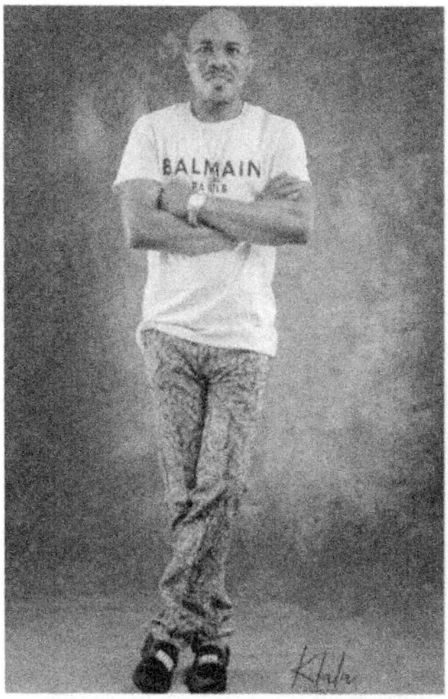
BALMAIN
Klala

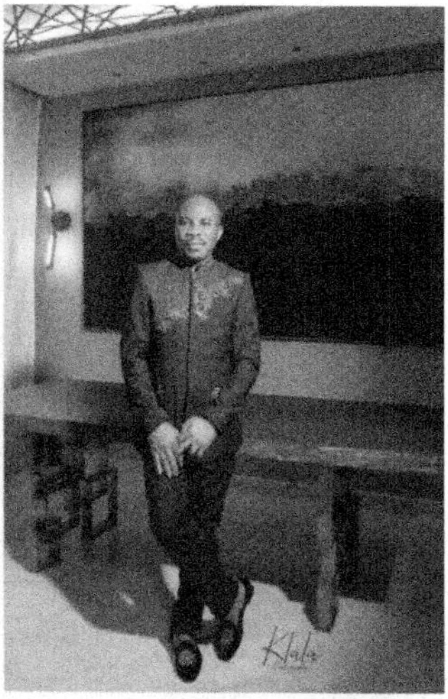
Klala

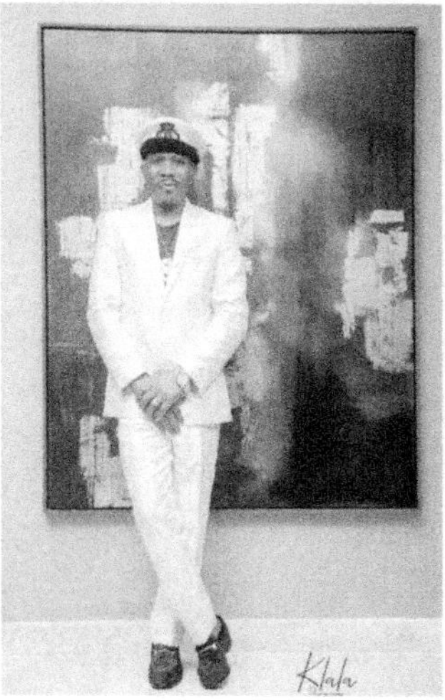
Klala

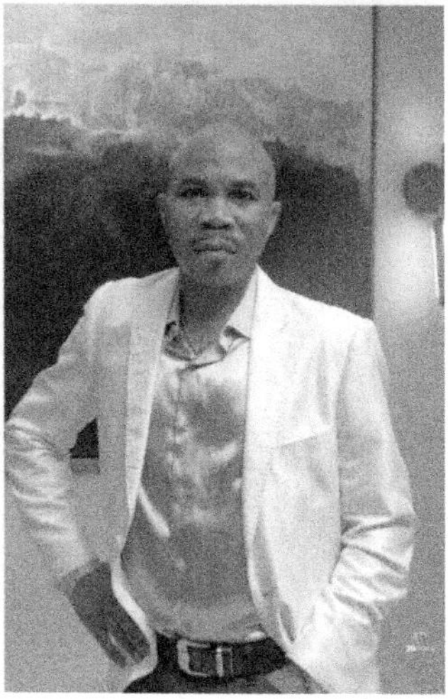

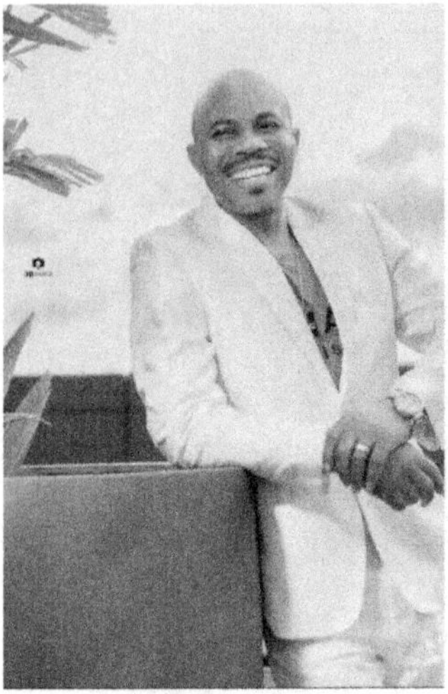

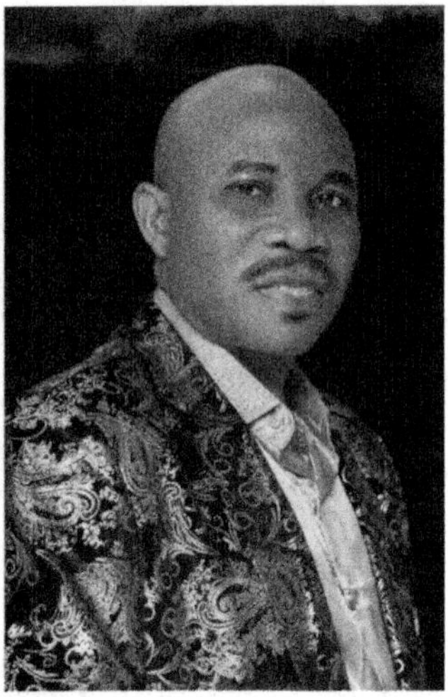

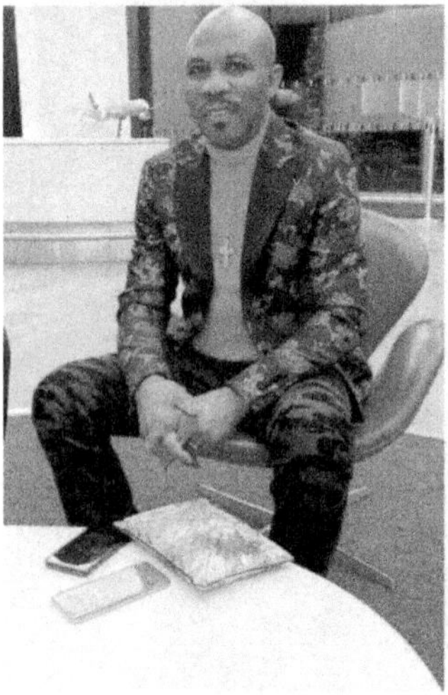

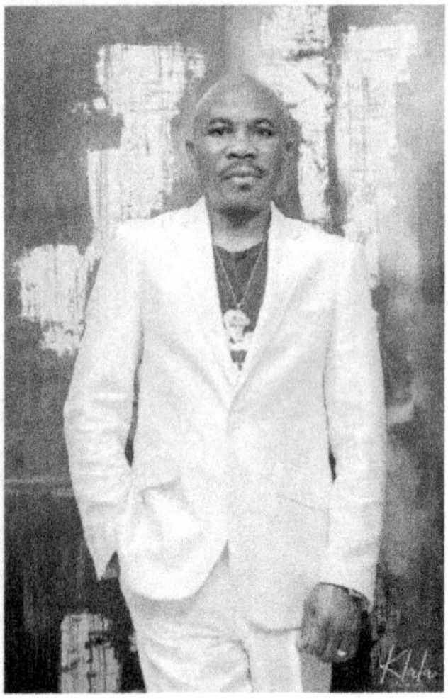